THE GENEROSITY SHIFT

HOW TITHING GROWS YOUR RELATIONSHIP WITH GOD

DR. SCOTT SILVERII

Five
Stones
Press

First Edition

Publisher: Five Stones Press, Dallas, Texas

For quantity sales, textbooks, and orders by trade bookstores or wholesalers contact Five Stones Press at publish@fivestonespress.net

Five Stones Press is owned and operated by Five Stones Church, a nonprofit 501c3 religious organization. Press name and logo are trademarked. Contact publisher for use.

Dr. Scott Silverii's website is scottsilverii.com

Printed in the United States of America

I dedicate this work to our incredible FaithFam at Five Stones Church. You are a joy and a blessing. Thank you for allowing our family to truly live this life and the next with you.
BE DIFFERENT,
Scott

INTRODUCTION
YOUR JOURNEY TO FINANCIAL
FREEDOM THROUGH RELATIONSHIP

Tithing: From Resistance to Relationship

I'll confess. I was one of those believers who railed against the church every time someone mentioned the word tithe. I don't mean by simply rolling my eyes or tucking my wallet deeper into my pocket. My emotions were at the point, had I heard one more slick manipulation of Scripture used to slip another buck from my billfold, I was going to stand up and lead a revolution out of the sanctuary.

I decided I'd go one step better than a rowdy exodus. I'd scrub Scripture until I'd unlocked every counter-argument to defeat those creepy church crawlers after my cold cash. Armed with a newfound battle cry, I'd proudly squash every call for tithes and offerings with, "That was under the law." Man, I was so right and so righteous, I should've received some humanitarian award for self-righteousness.

What I received was a taste of my own medicine just a few years later. Little did I know that guy on the platform would one day be me. I belabored through repetitive social media posts about how the tithe was outdated and not applicable. The cycle of refurbished chatter I'd heard and adopted as my own doctrine of financial freedom came back to bite me in the offering basket.

Then God flipped my world upside down.

This book offers a fresh perspective on tithing as a pathway to deeper relationship with God, based on my own transformation from skeptic to believer. It's the raw account of how God transformed my understanding of tithing from an obligation I resisted to a revelation of relationship I couldn't live without. What makes this journey different is that I've stood firmly on both sides of the tithing debate—and discovered that most of what is taught misses the truth of what God is after—your heart.

The Road Map: Your Journey Through This Book

In the pages ahead, you'll discover a fundamentally different approach to tithing—one built on relationship rather than religious obligation. To help you navigate this journey, here's what you can expect:

SECTION ONE: UNDERSTANDING TITHING

Chapter 1: Breaking Financial Chains—Discover the true purpose behind God's tithing system and why it's about relationship, not rules.

Chapter 2: The Tithe Is God's Trust Test—Learn how tithing serves as a spiritual barometer that reveals what's truly happening in your heart.

Chapter 3: Resisting Satan's Deceptions to Preserve God's Blessings—Explore how the enemy works to separate you from God's financial blessings.

SECTION TWO: OVERCOMING RESISTANCE

Chapter 4: Faith Over Fear—Confront the real reasons most Christians resist tithing and find freedom from financial anxiety.

Chapter 5: The Principle of First—Understand the transformative power of giving God your first and best, not your leftovers.

Chapter 6: The Principle of First—Giving That Lasts— See how consecrating your firstfruits changes everything that follows.

SECTION THREE: IMPLEMENTING FAITHFUL GIVING

Chapter 7: Walking in Freedom—Experience practical steps to break materialism's hold and live in God's favor.

Chapter 8: Let's Get Serious About Cheerful Giving— Move beyond the tithe to a lifestyle of generosity that reflects God's character.

Throughout this journey, you'll find:

• **Practical Assessment Tools** to evaluate your current relationship with money

- 🔍 **Biblical Deep Dives** that explore the rich historical and cultural context of tithing
- 💬 **Real-Life Testimonies** from people who have experienced God's provision through faithful tithing
- ☑️ **Action Steps** that help you implement these principles immediately
- ❓ **Reflection Questions** that prompt deeper spiritual growth

The Relationship-Trust-Blessing Framework

At the core of this book is a simple but profound framework that can transform how you view tithing:

The Relationship-Trust-Blessing Cycle

1.RELATIONSHIP: Tithing begins with understanding that God wants your connection, not your contribution. Every financial decision either strengthens or weakens your relationship with God.

2.TRUST: Through the act of tithing, you demonstrate trust in God's provision. This trust becomes the foundation for spiritual growth in all areas.

3.BLESSING: As you honor God with your firstfruits, He releases blessing—not just financially, but in every dimension of life through relationship.

4.INCREASED CAPACITY: These blessings expand your capacity for both receiving and giving, which deepens your relationship with God, completing and continuing the cycle of multiplication.

This cycle isn't a prosperity formula—it's a Scripture-based relationship principle. Each component builds on the others, creating an upward spiral of spiritual maturity and financial freedom.

Why This Book Now?

In a time when anxiety is at an all-time high and trust in religious institutions continues to decline, the subject of tithing has never been more contentious—or more necessary to understand correctly. I prepared this book to offer:

•An honest framework that addresses the strongest theological arguments for and against tithing

•A practical pathway to move from financial fear to supernatural provision

•A clear distinction between religious obligation and covenant relationship

•A Scripture-based structure that has transformed not only my family, but those of many others in the body of Christ. Whether you're a lifelong tither, a passionate skeptic, or somewhere in between, these pages will challenge your assumptions and offer a fresh, biblical perspective on what happens when we align our finances with God's relational principles.

What follows isn't a get-rich formula—it's an invitation to experience God at His Word. The windows of heaven are waiting to be unlocked. The key is in your hand.

This is simply about freedom—freedom from the anxiety of financial uncertainty, freedom from religious manipulation, freedom from the grip of materialism, and freedom to experience God's abundant provision simply according to His own Word.

My prayer is that as you read, you'll be challenged, encouraged, and ultimately transformed by the truth of God's Word regarding this vital aspect of our faith journey toward an active relationship with our Father.

The Kingdom Order Principle

The kingdom of God is a system of governance, and like any system, there are rules, structures, and order to all things. This is not to stop us from living a best blessed life.

I enjoy sharing the example with our faith family at Five Stones Church that Leah and I love driving to Biloxi for a few days of fresh seafood suppers. But to make the eight-hour drive from Texas requires I drive according to the laws and rules of the road. That does not stop us from a great getaway. The established order helps to make sure we arrive.

God's order is for our protection and provision. As citizens of heaven (Heavicans), we are responsible for learning biblical stewardship.

Freedom is understanding that loving God is not based on what He can do for you, but simply because of who He is. He is the sovereign holy God of creation, and as a co-heir of King Jesus, I am sharing the truth of what it means, what is required, and what will result from your walking in a true reverent fear of the Lord.

When we learn that loving God is not based upon fickle emotions, but on honor and obedience, we begin to understand the depth of His unwavering, sacrificial love for us.

I also understand that this can make a relationship with God sound a little stiff and programmatic, but growing intimacy with God must first start with a healthy, holy honor. John 14:15 helps us start that deep connection by sharing, "If you love Me, keep My commandments" (NKJV).

I explain it this way. Our kids love to joke around with me. The reason they have that access to an intimate, friendly interaction with me as their dad is because they first respect me as their father. It's the same way with God.

It's so important to understand the character of God so we don't build our own boxes within which we expect Him to perform. One of the elements for opening our eyes to Him is the tithe. This really is the truth test for whether our hearts are tied to Him, or to the material world. I'll give you a quick example below:

While we associate money with a worldly monetary value, God uses wealth to establish His covenant relationship with us.

"And you shall remember the Lord your God, for it is He who gives you power to get wealth, that He may establish His covenant which He swore to your fathers, as it is this day" (Deuteronomy 8:18 NKJV).

A great test of how deeply your heart is tethered to money is how this Scripture causes you to react. Any response outside of seeing God as your loving Father opens a great opportunity to move past the mistaken or manipulative teachings you've heard in the past. I pray this information guides you into understanding His love for you as it also frees you from the grip of monetary bondage.

The Four Core Principles of Biblical Financial-Driven Freedom

As you journey through this book, you'll discover four foundational principles that will transform your relationship with both God and money:

1. **The Principle of First**—God deserves our first and best, not our leftovers. When we honor Him with our firstfruits, He redeems and multiplies what remains.

2. **The Trust Test Principle**—Tithing reveals what we truly trust. It's God's divine barometer for measuring whether money has become an idol in our lives.

3. **The Consecration Principle**—Setting apart our tithe transforms it from currency to covenant—a sacred act that invites God's supernatural blessing.

4. **The Kingdom Order Principle**—God's financial system operates according to divine structure, not human

emotion or logic. Aligning with this order brings protection and provision.

These four principles will appear throughout the book, providing a consistent framework for understanding God's design for our finances.

Each principle builds upon the others, creating a comprehensive approach to tithing that transforms it from a religious duty to a relational delight.

God is calling you into a deeper relationship with Him. Your heart sets the pace of that race back to the Father. Obedient actions, not flowery words or empty intentions, measure your true heart for Him.

The tithe continues to serve as the litmus test for determining whether you love God or gold. Do you have a loving and generous character that reflects God? Do your actions match your words relative to your love for God?

If you long for a true, tangible encounter with the living God, please receive this well: God moves in atmospheres of holy, reverent fear. Before you move to Chapter 1, I've included a quick assessment to use as a guide on where you are on giving.

FINANCIAL HEART CHECK

Rate yourself 1–5 on each statement:

___I regularly review my bank statements

___I can name my three largest monthly expenses

___I have a written budget I follow

___I give consistently to my church

__I save money each month

__Money rarely causes stress in my relationships

SCORING:

24–30: Excellent stewardship foundation

18–23: Good foundation, room for growth

12–17: Significant improvement needed

Below 12: Time for major financial changes

SECTION ONE:
UNDERSTANDING TITHING

CHAPTER 1
BREAKING FINANCIAL CHAINS: OBEDIENCE BEYOND EMOTIONS
THE CALL TO DEEPER OBEDIENCE

I WAS in the second year of teaching a series through the gospel of Mark, but in my personal prayer time, Holy Spirit dropped a truth bomb about obedience. This revelation reminded me of the promises God made to Five Stones Church before we'd planted the church.

The Lord said He'd do a supernaturally significant work through the church if we'd simply obey Him. I was all in the first time He'd said that years ago. It had been an incredible journey up to this point in late 2024, yet I knew we had not even scratched the surface of His promise.

Were we still walking in faithful obedience? Had we, or I, been rebellious? To my relief, it wasn't as much about a lack of obedience as it was a new season of going deeper into understanding and obeying His commands.

WITH MORE GIVEN, there is more expected. Those promises made to a fresh upstart church plant would require a new, more intimate understanding of what relationship with God the Father looked like.

SPIRITUAL INSIGHT: Obedience isn't a one-time decision but a progressive journey of moving from glory to glory. As we grow in faith, God calls us to deeper levels of trust and surrender.

Leah and I have always prayed, "Whatever, whenever, wherever, we will follow," and it was now the season to act upon that prayer. Immediate obedience is my superpower only because I know that if I linger or debate about it, I'll default to inactivity. In other words—disobedience.

I know this can be a hard truth, but delayed obedience is disobedience. So just like that, I plunged into the one area I had once rebelled against and thanks be to God, was delivered from: the Tithe.

But wasn't I the guy who once proclaimed, "I'll never tithe?" Yes, and doesn't God have a wonderful sense of humor? All the previous years of digging deep into Scripture to disprove the current relevancy of the tithe would become the seeds God used to blossom the correction of understanding and a stronger connection to Him.

Remaining teachable and open to correction is vital to a healthy relationship with God. When the Lord speaks to His church, He uses encouragement and correction. Five Stones Church would be no different than the way He addressed the seven churches in the Book of Revelation. This is what I shared from my teaching notes that first Sunday:

God's instructions to His church include a balance of encouragement and correction.

So which news do you want first?

Here's the encouragement: *God is pleased that we are a house of prayer and worship. He loves that we are BOLD to move freely in the gifts of the Holy Spirit.*

Here's the correction: *We are not obedient to His command to tithe. This message is not about money; it's about your relationship with God. It's about trusting Him in all areas of your life. It is about going deeper into knowing Him.*

The Principle of First: Tithing as Relationship, Not Religion

In 2 Corinthians 3:18, the Bible says as we "are being transformed into the same image from glory to glory," we learn to be more Christlike as we press into our relationship with Him. Just as I learned His truth about the tithe, we are all called to reflect more of Him and less of ourselves.

The process of sanctification is indeed a process, and our church was growing into a deeper level of obedience. We were covering the bases as we matured into our third year as a faith-filled body, but we were sort of lingering between third base and home plate. If I can use the analogy as I saw it, the Holy Spirit was the third base coach waving us to charge home plate and score a winning run.

To go where the Lord wanted to take the corporate body would require sacrifice that went deeper than the five-week water fast I committed to while receiving this revelation on obedience.

I knew the only ethical way to share God's word about obedience was to share what His Holy Word had to say about it. This is what I'm sharing with you and why I am following my sermon notes as the pathway of the three-week series I used to teach it.

Many modern churches become overly concerned with getting feet off the street and into the seat to pay for their new stadium-sized arenas with coffee bars and smoke machines. They avoid hard topics that might possibly make new congregants uncomfortable. Between the false doctrines that satiate the emotions and the proof texting of Scripture that manipulates money matters, it's a wonder anyone has a correct understanding of tithing.

The Historical Context of Tithing

To fully appreciate God's design for tithing, we must understand its rich historical context. Tithing wasn't invented as a fundraising mechanism for the modern consumer social congregation—its roots are deep in ancient covenant practices.

Unlike pagan cultures where tithes were often extracted through fear, the biblical tithe was designed as a relational practice—a way of honoring God that strengthened the covenant between Him and His people.

Tithing Before the Law

One of the most common "out clauses" Christians use to keep their cash is claiming the tithe was Old Testament law and we are now under the covenant of grace. I'm all about you having the free will to do what you want with your money, but I'm even more about you having the facts before you exercise that freedom.

The tithe predates the Mosaic law by centuries. Abraham's tithe to Melchizedek occurred about 430 years before the law was given.

"Then Melchizedek king of Salem brought out bread and wine; he was the priest of God Most High. And he blessed him and said:

'Blessed be Abram of God Most High,

Possessor of heaven and earth;

And blessed be God Most High,

Who has delivered your enemies into your hand.'

And he gave him a tithe of all" (Genesis 14:18–20 NKJV).

This wasn't a response to a command but a spontaneous act of honor and relationship.

Jacob's vow to tithe similarly came hundreds of years before the law.

"Then Jacob made a vow, saying, 'If God will be with me, and keep me in this way that I am going, and give me bread to eat and clothing to put on, so that I come back to my father's house in peace, then the Lord shall be my God. And this stone which I have set as a pillar shall be God's house, and of all that You give me I will surely give a tenth to You'" (Genesis 28:20–22 NKJV).

We will examine both Scriptures later in the book, but I wanted to illustrate that tithing is a timeless principle of relationship with God, not merely a legal requirement.

Tithing in Temple and Synagogue Practice

By the time Jesus came to walk with us on earth, tithing had evolved into a structured practice within Judaism. The temple system depended on tithes for its operation, and local synagogues were supported through community contributions. Jesus never abolished this practice; instead, He addressed the heart behind it.

"Woe to you, scribes and Pharisees, hypocrites! For you pay tithe of mint and anise and cummin and have neglected the weightier matters of the law: justice and mercy and faith. These you ought to have done, without leaving the others undone" (Matthew 23:23 NKJV).

When Jesus criticized the Pharisees' tithing of "mint, dill, and cumin," He wasn't dismissing the practice of tithing but rather highlighting that they had maintained the practice while neglecting "the weightier matters of the law—justice, mercy and faithfulness." His instruction was to do better. To do both!

What Would the Church Think?

It was an abrupt transition from a weekly study of Mark and into a teaching about obedience to God. What would our church feel about this sudden shift? Honestly, I had an assignment from the Lord, and because I love the congregation, I had no choice but to remain honest and open with them.

I did what any obedient person would do—I announced that we as the corporate body had not yet become as obedient as the Lord desired. I sought His direction for affirmation, and He gave this Scripture:

"Likewise, the Spirit also helps in our weaknesses. For we do not know what we should pray for as we ought, but the Spirit Himself makes intercession for us with groanings which cannot be uttered" (Romans 8:26 NKJV).

Why the Intercession Urgency?

The Lord had given a clear promise from day one, that He would use the church as a light to the dark world and to the lukewarm churches. He'd allowed us the first few years to learn the ropes of church governance, team building and the many areas of help and hinderance of planting and shepherding His church.

Besides, I'd left the only career I'd known as an adult when I walked away in my twenty-sixth year and retired as a police chief to serve only the Lord. My first sermon on launch day, was my first sermon ever. Yes, I had a lot to learn.

During this same season of the Lord leading us into a true understanding of relational, reverent fear, the country was experiencing a shaking and exposure of celebrity pastors, megachurches, and television ministries for everything from sexual sin to financial fraud. God was actively removing the man-made veil of compromise that had been drawn over institutionalized religion.

God will not be mocked and, whether we were a church of ten or ten thousand, the standard of righteousness does not waver.

"For the eyes of the Lord run to and fro throughout the whole earth, to show Himself strong on behalf of those whose heart is loyal to Him" (2 Chronicles 16:9a NKJV).

God was groaning to use Five Stones Church as that example of His righteousness. Our collective ability to move into a deeper relationship with God hinged on our willingness and desire to follow His commands. The tangible tool God uses for obeying His commands starts with honoring the tithe.

I know this is a point of departure for some Christians who sigh, "Money grab," beneath bated breath, but that is expected. Some may question the church's motives in teaching about tithing. I understand this concern because I once felt the same way. It was also the exact reason the Lord chose the tithe now just as He did from the start to reveal the true condition of our heart.

The Trust Test Principle in Action

You see, we all tithe. The question is, "Who are you tithing to?"

Most people if they're willing to be honest, tithe to their gods (super lowercase "g") of the world. Their daily specialty coffees, video games and hi-tech electronics, their unused gym memberships, internet and cable subscription services, and not to mention vanity spending on high-priced tennis shoes and entertainment tickets, all add up to placing their worship of distraction above their focused worship of God.

In the summer of 2024, I watched in shock as a female pop singer's concert tickets cost over eight hundred dollars and up to several thousand per show. My social media feed was littered with parents posting about bringing their kids and friends and how much they invested in a lifetime core memory.

I'm not knocking it. I remember dropping a whole seven dollars back in the eighties to see Cheap Trick on a college campus after I used a friend's student ID to get the discounted price.

God wants you to have money. God does not want money to have you. I can say that because I know what God says about provisions.

"And this same God who takes care of me will supply all your needs from his glorious riches, which have been given to us in Christ Jesus" (Philippians 4:19 NLT).

Tithing and Spiritual Disciplines

Tithing doesn't exist in isolation—it's interconnected with other spiritual disciplines that shape our character and deepen our relationship with God. Consider how tithing relates to these essential practices:

Prayer

Just as prayer opens communication with God, tithing opens our hearts to trust Him with our material resources and needs. Both practices require faith that God hears and responds to our actions.

Fasting

Fasting denies physical appetites to focus on spiritual nourishment. Similarly, tithing denies our material appetites (the desire to keep everything for ourselves) to nurture spiritual growth. Both practices say, "God, I want You more than what sustains me physically."

Worship

True worship acknowledges God's worth and sovereignty. Tithing is a tangible expression of worship that declares God's ownership of everything we have. Both elevate God above ourselves.

Bible Study

Scripture study transforms our minds to think like Christ. Tithing transforms our relationship with material possessions to align with God's values. Both reshape our worldview to reflect kingdom priorities.

When practiced together, these disciplines create a holistic approach to spiritual formation that touches every dimension of our lives—heart, soul, mind, and strength. The tithe becomes not an isolated financial transaction but part of an integrated lifestyle of devotion to God.

REFLECTION QUESTION: Which spiritual discipline do you find easiest to practice? Which is most challenging? How might strengthening your practice of tithing affect your engagement with other spiritual disciplines?

One challenge I faced in teaching the series to the church the first time was breaking off the misunderstanding and bad teaching that we are no longer under any obligation to the Old Testament. Whoever planted that seed in believers' brains has buried it deep and did a great disservice to the eternal truth of God's Word.

Scripture like Deuteronomy 8:18 and the many other promises of God should excite believers.

Instead, they dismiss a direct word from Him with a claim of, "That's Old Testament and it doesn't apply to me. I'm under the blood of Christ."

God's Word is not a salad bar that you get to pick what you like and toss the rest. We should be grateful for every word from:

"In the beginning God created the heavens and the earth" (Genesis 1:1 NLT)

to

"May the grace of the Lord Jesus be with God's holy people" (Revelation 22:21 NLT).

All of God's Word is important.

We are people of covenant. How do we know what applied then applies to us now?

"So, the promise is received by faith. It is given as a gift.

And we are all certain to receive it, whether we live according to the law of Moses, if we have faith like Abraham's. For Abraham is the father of all who believe" (Romans 4:16 NLT). Through faith, we become spiritual descendants of Abraham. We inherit God's promises—including provision. We also remain under the command to follow God's commands.

Chapter Summary: The Four Key Takeaways

1.**The Trust Test Principle**—Tithing serves as God's divine test to reveal what truly has our heart—Him or material possessions.

2.**Tithing Is Relational, Not Religious**—God established tithing as a means of deepening our relationship with Him, not as a fundraising mechanism.

3.**Spiritual Disciplines Work Together**—Tithing connects with prayer, fasting, worship, and Bible study to form a complete picture of devotion to God.

4.**Obedience Precedes Understanding**—Sometimes we must obey God's commands before we fully understand their purpose, trusting that His ways are higher than ours.

Glossary of Key Terms

Tithe: The word literally means "tenth" or "one-tenth." In biblical context, it refers to giving the first 10 percent of one's increase back to God.

Firstfruits: The first and best portion of one's harvest or increase, offered to God as a recognition of His provision and ownership.

Storehouse: In Malachi 3:10, refers to the temple treasury. For contemporary believers, typically understood as the local church where you receive spiritual nourishment.

Principle of First: The biblical concept that God deserves our first and best, not our leftovers. This applies to time, talent, and treasure.

Consecration: From the Hebrew word "qadash," meaning "to set apart as holy." When applied to tithing, it refers to dedicating the tithe as sacred and separate from ordinary use.

Covenant: A binding agreement between God and His people. Tithing is a covenant practice that acknowledges God's provision and our stewardship.

Devourer: Referenced in Malachi 3:11, represents forces that destroy financial increase. God promises to rebuke the devourer for those who tithe faithfully.

Stewardship: The biblical understanding that we don't own anything—we merely manage what God has entrusted to us.

Mammon: An Aramaic word referring to material wealth or possessions when they are treated as an idol or object of worship.

Kingdom Order: God's divine system of governance, including principles, structures, and commands that bring protection and blessing when followed.

CHAPTER 2
THE TITHE IS GOD'S TRUST TEST FOR RELATIONSHIPS

The Divine Barometer

God made His intention for abundant provision crystal clear from the very beginning. We cannot toss the Old Testament into the doctrinal garbage can. That's where so many Christians have lost their opportunities to honor and be blessed by God.

The Old Testament is precisely where God first spoke His eternal blessings of being fruitful and multiplying. Then Jesus echoed the relationship between multiplication and faith in the New Testament's Matthew 25:14–30 where He shares the parable of the five talents.

The master tells the servants who financially multiplied what was entrusted to them, "Well done, good and faithful servant; you have been faithful over a few things, I will make you ruler over many things. Enter into the joy of your lord" (Matthew 25:23 NKJV). This is Jesus' parable, not mine.

Take a quick peek at what the master said to the servant who hid their money: "You wicked and lazy servant..." Do you get the sense of God's never-wavering desire to bless us? What He spoke in the beginning is affirmed by Jesus because God does not change His heart for us. It's our hearts that have changed toward Him. The tithe is the test to reveal where our hearts are toward Him.

God's garden of Eden design was perfect by, well, design. God created it all and gave it all to us to care for and use as needed so that we thrived without want, need, or lack.

"Then God blessed them, and God said to them, 'Be fruitful and multiply; fill the earth and subdue it; have dominion over the fish of the sea, over the birds of the air, and over every living thing that moves on the earth'" (Genesis 1:28 NKJV).

I always ask the church, so I'll ask you: Show me Scripture where God said this is no longer His desire for you? God deeply wants this state of perfection in His relationship with you restored.

Right after humanity sinned and gave ownership of God's perfect creation to Satan, He immediately declared the plan of redemption. The price God was willing to pay as a ransom to get it back for you was His beloved Son, Jesus.

"And I will put enmity
Between you and the woman,

And between your seed and her Seed;

He shall bruise your head,

And you shall bruise His heel" (Genesis 3:15 NKJV).

Do you think God would have sacrificed His only begotten Son if everything He'd done before crucifixion and resurrection no longer mattered? If we make any progress up to this point, I trust it's to gain an appreciation for the full counsel of God's Word.

Coming to receive His complete Word as true and eternal will leave no pieces of the puzzle missing and your application of His will for your life complete.

I will share that during the years I spent looking for loopholes to justify my resistance to the tithe, I came to know Scripture from start and finish. A full understanding of the counsel of God unlocks the understanding of God's character and desire for our lives. It's from that understanding of who He is and how He loves us that I share with you.

Biblical Obedience: Relationship Through Covenant

Let's move forward to unlock God's blessings. The tithe is a foundational principle for honoring God through obedience. This is a great time to talk about what is biblical obedience. I've discovered Christians interject their feelings into certain words in Scripture with what they feel it should mean according to what suits them best.

Words like submission, sacrifice, and obedience cause a quick recoil and sometimes dismissal before truth is received. So, let's clear up and understand exactly what is meant by obedience.

From a biblical perspective, the Hebrew context of obedience is deeply rooted in the covenant relationship between God and His people. The Hebrew word for obedience is "shema," which means "to hear" or "to listen." This word carries the implication of not just hearing but also responding appropriately to what is heard.

HEBREW INSIGHT: The word "shema" (שְׁמַע) is both about hearing and responding. It implies attentive listening that leads to action. When God commands and we "shema," we're not just acknowledging His voice—we're aligning our lives with His instruction.

Here are some key aspects of biblical obedience from a Hebrew perspective:

1. Covenant Relationship

God's promises and the people's commitment to follow His commandments are found, for example, in Exodus 19:4–6:

'You have seen what I did to the Egyptians. You know how I carried you on eagles' wings and brought you to myself. Now if you will obey me and keep my covenant, you will be my own special treasure from among all the peoples on earth; for all the earth belongs to me. And you will be my kingdom of priests, my holy nation.' This is the message you must give to the people of Israel." (NLT)

THIS ISN'T a cold contract of demands and obligations. It's a loving invitation into special relationship—becoming God's "treasured possession" among all peoples. The Hebrew term "segullah" (treasured possession) conveys something of extraordinary value, cherished and protected.

2. Shema Prayer

One of the most significant expressions of obedience in the Hebrew context is found in the Shema prayer, which begins with Deuteronomy 6:4–5:

"Hear, O Israel: The Lord our God, the Lord is one. Love the Lord your God with all your heart and with all your soul and with all your strength" (NIV)

This prayer emphasizes the importance of loving and obeying God wholeheartedly. It begins with "Hear" (Shema) —a call to listen with the intent to respond in faithful obedience.

3. Prophetic Call to Obedience

The Hebrew prophets frequently called the people of Israel to return to obedience to God's commandments. For instance, the prophet Micah sums up what the Lord requires:

"He has shown you, O mortal, what is good. And what does the Lord require of you? To act justly and to love mercy and to walk humbly with your God" (Micah 6:8 NIV).

This verse beautifully captures that obedience isn't only about rigid rule-following but about character alignment with God's nature—justice, mercy, and humility. If you recall

Jesus' rebuke and correction of the Pharisees in Matthew 23:23, where He reaffirms this instruction.

4. Blessings and Curses

In Deuteronomy, blessings for obedience and curses for disobedience are clearly outlined. Deuteronomy 28 describes the blessings that will come if Israel obeys God and the curses that will come if they do not. This highlights the importance of obedience in maintaining the covenant relationship and experiencing God's favor.

5. Heart and Actions

In the Hebrew context, obedience is not just about external actions but also about the condition of the heart. 1 Samuel 15:22 highlights this when Samuel says: "But Samuel replied, "What is more pleasing to the Lord: your burnt offerings and sacrifices or your obedience to his voice? Listen! Obedience is better than sacrifice, and submission is better than offering the fat of rams. (NLT)

This verse emphasizes that true obedience comes from a heart that seeks to align with God's will.

"Today the Lord your God has commanded you to obey all these decrees and regulations. So be careful to obey them wholeheartedly" (Deuteronomy 26:16 NLT).

These are just a few examples for illustrating relationship with God, our holy sovereign Father, is grounded in obedience and not the sway of fickle emotion.

THE TRUST TEST: **Revealing Your Heart's True Condition**

The one thing Holy Spirit stressed as I prepared that sermon series and now this book is the tithe is God's trust test for relationships. This is an important reality because either you trust God to provide for you by bringing Him your tithe, or you trust worldly wealth and materialism as your god. Because God loves you so dearly, you are free to choose, but dear friend, choose wisely.

REFLECTION QUESTION: If someone examined your bank statements for the past three months, what would they conclude was most important to you? Would there be evidence of regular tithing? Or would all spending be centered on yourself?

"Do you trust God?" is a question of self-reflection you should always be willing to ask and more importantly, answer honestly. I'll tell you there were times in my life where I did not completely trust God. On one occasion, Holy Spirit asked me that very direct question, "Do you trust Me?" and I angrily replied, "Ninety-nine point nine percent."

In what I can only describe as the mercy of God's holy conviction, He whispered, "That's not enough." Following that, I faithfully investigated the source of that 0.1 percent, and why it kept me at a distance from my Father.

It was fear.

I had already given so much (or so I thought), that when I did not see the results I expected, I began to fear God was not going to uphold His part of the promise. Instead of resentment, I repented and grew to love and embrace the lesson from Mark 12:41–44.

The Widow's Two Mites

"Now Jesus sat opposite the treasury and saw how the people put money into the treasury. And many who were rich put in much. Then one poor widow came and threw in two mites, which make a quadrans.

So He called His disciples to Himself and said to them, 'Assuredly, I say to you that this poor widow has put in more than all those who have given to the treasury; for they all put in out of their abundance, but she out of her poverty put in all that she had, her whole livelihood'" (NKJV)

It wasn't about how much the widow gave; it was from what that she did give. She gave her whole livelihood. That meant from all it took for her to live on. Yes, even her gym membership and premium television channels, she gave it all.

Do you think she was giving out of happy feelings? No. She was moved by obedience and love, and God honored that because if she was that faithful, it was not the first or only time the widow gave her whole livelihood. Yet each week, God provided for her that same way He wants to provide for you.

The Trust Test in My Life: A Personal Testimony

I'll share some of my backstory, so you better understand what I meant when I said earlier that I had already given up so much. I was in my twenty-sixth year of law enforcement and a current chief of police. I was also a college professor at night and contracted as a subject matter expert for the federal government. In the natural realm, I was crushing it.

I had just been confirmed with another four-year term as chief that would bring me to a comfortable full thirty-year pension. That meant I'd receive 100 percent of my highest paid years as my pension, and my health insurance paid the rest of my life.

When God called me to walk away and serve only Him, He said, "You spent your career locking men up. Now live your life setting them free." Two weeks later, I was a civilian for the first time in my adult life.

He even wanted me to surrender the college teaching and government contracting—everything. So yes, I understand what the widow tossed in that basket when she "put in all that she had, her whole livelihood."

I thought I'd given up more than my fair share and had an edge about God's level of commitment to the agreement. Oh, but I had no idea that in what I saw as my poverty, how much more there was to give to the Lord.

Does God want to show His love for you through provision? Yes, but do you trust Him? It's okay to answer with a no. This is your chance to break free from a poverty mindset. If you do answer with a no, you are not alone. Many Christians struggle with tithing to the church as God desires.

WHY CHRISTIANS DON'T TITHE: Confronting the Real Barriers

The top three reasons Christians do not tithe, offer, or give is that they are confused about what the Bible says about tithes and offerings, they don't trust church leadership with their money, and they do not believe Old Testament Scriptures apply to them.

The foundation behind each of these reasons stem from the devil's lies and manipulations. I'm not suggesting some churches haven't mismanaged money, or pastors and leaders have not pilfered the pulpit.

These sins are egregious, but do not allow the devil to turn you away from all that God has for you. This is not about the church and your money. This is about your personal relationship with God the Father.

Barrier #1: Confusion About Biblical Teaching

Many Christians have heard conflicting teachings about tithing, often presented without proper Scriptural context. This confusion leads to paralysis—if you're not sure what's right, it's easier to do nothing.

The Truth: The Bible provides clear, consistent teaching about tithing throughout both Testaments. When we examine the full counsel of Scripture, the principle of giving God our first and best emerges as a timeless truth.

Barrier #2: Lack of Trust in Church Leadership

Unfortunately, financial scandals and mismanagement

have damaged trust in religious institutions. Some believers use these failures as justification to withhold their tithe.

The Truth: Your tithe is ultimately given to God, not to a person or organization. While wise stewardship includes ensuring your local church handles finances with integrity, the command to tithe is about your relationship with God, not your evaluation of church leadership.

I'd like to suggest that instead of criticizing church leaders, that you pray about offering help in terms of serving in areas that promote financial accountability.

Barrier #3: Rejection of Old Testament Principles

Many Christians have been taught that Old Testament practices no longer apply under the New Covenant of grace. This view selectively applies to financial commands while maintaining other Old Testament moral teachings.

The Truth: Jesus didn't abolish the law but fulfilled it (Matthew 5:17–18). The principles established in the Old Testament continue to reveal God's character and expectations. Tithing began before the law (with Abraham and Jacob) and was affirmed by Jesus in the New Testament.

Also, refusing to honor God with your tithe should not be driven by feelings for the pastor. If you legitimately can't trust the church you attend with your money, you sure shouldn't trust it to faithfully minister the Word of God.

Finally, there should be no confusion when it comes to God's Word. I want to address whatever your reason may be for not tithing. It's not financial—it's relational.

In the next chapter, let's keep it real as we explore who wants to come between your relationship with God more than anyone.

Chapter Summary: The Four Key Takeaways

1.**The Trust Test Reveals Our Heart**—Tithing exposes whether we truly trust God or rely on our own provision.

2.**Biblical Obedience Is Relational**—The Hebrew concept of "shema" shows that obedience is about responsive relationship, not rigid religion.

3.**Fear Often Masquerades as Theology**—Many objections to tithing are rooted in fear rather than biblical understanding.

4.**Tithing Is About Surrender**—Like the widow's mites, tithing demonstrates our willingness to surrender everything to God.

CHAPTER 3
RESISTING SATAN'S DECEPTIONS TO PRESERVE GOD'S BLESSINGS
THE CASE AGAINST SATAN

ONE CHALLENGE as I steward my role as pastor is sharing the reality that anything turning you away from God is not of God. Anything not of God has two options: our flesh (Galatians 5:17) or Satan.

The balance I must find also means not necessarily categorizing a refusal to tithe as demonic, with the only solution being deliverance. It could also be a matter of ignorance and/or deception. So, with that in mind, let me walk you through the process of discernment as revealed in God's Scripture.

One of the biggest challenges is untangling Satan's deceptions. All Satan can do is counterfeit what God creates by killing, stealing, and destroying the beauty of God's handiwork. He's twisted Scripture to create a false love for materialism and a resistance to honoring God through tithing.

Another question I asked the church, so I'll ask you, "Who made you believe tithing was optional?" If God calls us to tithe, wouldn't it make sense at the very base level to follow His call?

The Ancient Strategy: Separating Us from God's Blessing

Satan's strategy hasn't changed since the garden of Eden. His primary goal is to separate us from God and His blessings. In Genesis 3:1, he used a simple question to plant doubt: "Did God really say...?"

He continues to use this same tactic regarding tithing, whispering questions that make us doubt God's commands and intentions.

The enemy knows that financial obedience is a powerful connector to God's blessing, so he works tirelessly to break this connection through:

1.**Sowing confusion** about biblical teaching on tithing

2.**Promoting fear** that you won't have enough if you tithe

3.**Encouraging self-reliance** rather than God-dependence

4.**Stirring resentment** toward church leadership

5.**Twisting Scripture** to justify disobedience

SPIRITUAL WARFARE INSIGHT: Satan doesn't attack areas of your life that pose no threat to his agenda. The fierce opposition many feel toward tithing reveals its spiritual significance. The enemy fights hardest against practices that most powerfully connect us to God's blessing.

A Call to Love and Obedience

"And now, Israel, what does the Lord your God require of you? He requires only that you fear the Lord your God, and live in a way that pleases him, and love him and serve him with all your heart and soul. And you must always obey the Lord's commands and decrees that I am giving you today for your own good" (Deuteronomy 10:12–13 NLT).

Yet, many Christians become primal in their attacks against the mention of honoring God by offering the tithe. By and large Christians are divided on everything from salvation to abortion, but the one thing most rally around is keeping control of their cash. Does that seem like the heart of the Father or a little self-serving rebellion?

God created the tithe as a simple tool to make sure nothing stands between your heart and Him. Can you see why Satan must convince Christians that the tithe is an irrelevant concept based on outdated Scriptures?

The tithe is not about financing fancy churches; it's about ensuring God is your priority. The issue with churches not teaching unfiltered Scripture is that it causes Christians to turn their wrath against God and not the god of this world who blocks their blessings—Satan.

"Satan, who is the god of this world, has blinded the minds of those who don't believe. They are unable to see the glorious light of the Good News. They don't understand this message about the glory of Christ, who is the exact likeness of God" (2 Corinthians 4:4 NLT).

Blinded by the Enemy: How Satan Obscures God's Blessing

My heart in sharing this truth based on Scripture is to help you unlock God's abundant blessings. Trusting God's Word corrects this demonic case of misinformation! If you don't think so, ask yourself, "What is listening to Satan costing me?"

When your heart clings to anything but God, you repeat Adam and Eve's mistake—you hand over to Satan all authority and dominion God intended for you.

"So, the Lord God banished them from the Garden of Eden, and he sent Adam out to cultivate the ground from which he had been made" (Genesis 3:23 NLT).

Satan only has one trick. He used it in the garden, and he continues using it against God's people. How does he do it? The way he used a piece of fruit to separate Adam and Eve from God, he now uses money to destroy your relationship with the Father also.

"Did God really say that?" is all it takes to plant a seed of doubt that bears the fruit of discord. That slight sleight of hand and we treat God's tithe like an option to tip a waitress at the restaurant. Tithing isn't optional.

It was established about 430 years before Mosaic law and continues today, as I've shared through Scripture and will go into more detail in the following chapters. Don't let Satan rob you of God's blessings. Obey and trust God by tithing.

"No one can serve two masters; for either he will hate the one and love the other, or else he will be loyal to the one and despise the other. You cannot serve God and mammon" (Matthew 6:24 NKJV).

The Spirit of Mammon: Understanding Your Real Enemy

For clarity, mammon refers to wealth, money, or material possessions. It's often referred to as an evil spirit. When Jesus teaches against mammon, He is emphasizing the choice between spiritual devotion and the pursuit and love of wealth.

Mammon symbolizes the idolization of material wealth, and the moral pitfalls associated with prioritizing worldly riches over spiritual values. Simply put, mammon is greed.

Greed opposes generosity like Satan opposes God. Choose this day who shall you serve. You cannot serve both. God's desire is for a surrendered heart, not a heart bent on pursuing material wealth.

The Cultural and Historical Context of Mammon

The term "mammon" has deeper significance than many realize. In Jesus' day, it wasn't just about money—it represented an entire system opposed to God's kingdom values:

Ancient Near Eastern Background

In ancient Aramaic culture, Mammon was personified as a deity or demonic entity associated with wealth and materialism. When Jesus used this term, His audience would have understood the stark spiritual implications—choosing between God and an opposing spiritual force.

The Idolatry Connection

The worship of wealth wasn't abstract in the ancient world. Temples to gods of prosperity and wealth polluted the landscape. Christians were called to reject these cultural norms and embrace countercultural generosity.

Modern Applications

Today's consumer culture has created sophisticated systems of mammon-worship that are often more subtle but equally powerful. Credit systems, advertising, status symbols, and consumer debt all serve to entangle us in mammon's web. Tithing stands as a deliberate act of righteous rebellion against this cultural current.

I like to use what we call Equipping Moments during sermons. They are practical life applications of God's Word. A challenge I propose to you for getting a factual and tangible assessment of who or what is most important in your life is to try this exercise below. Our best lessons come from our own experiences.

Equipping Moment: The Bank Statement Revelation

The purpose of tithing is to reveal who you truly serve. At some point take a break from reading this book and look at your bank account. My example was first to the body of Five Stones Church, but you know from which local church you are fed spiritually. In Scripture, that would be your storehouse.

God's invitation in Malachi 3:10 to "test me in this" demonstrates His confidence in His provision. Do tithes and giving to your church show up on your bank account register of expenditures?

This is not to condemn you, but it should serve the purpose for which God applied it, and that is to convict you of what is truly most important in your life. Your spending shows what's important to you.

"For where your treasure is, there your heart will be also" (Matthew 6:21 NKJV).

There's nothing wrong with enjoying Starbucks, video games, or eating out at fine-dining restaurants—but not at the expense of your relationship with God. We all tithe to something. The question is, which god are you tithing to?

So many Christians claim to love God and live for Him, but unless their words are supported by truth in action, it would be better to say nothing at all. This is one of several Scriptures that are completely transparent about God seeing those who say one thing but do another.

"They profess to know God, but in works they deny Him, being abominable, disobedient, and disqualified for every good work" (Titus 1:16 NKJV).

BREAKING the Stronghold of Financial Deception

This is not my idea, but I'm glad it's my reality. I'm simply sharing God's Word——trusting it will bring you into alignment, so God can increase His blessing upon you, the body and His church. God asks for His tenth. Satan demands it all. Satan has done a masterful job at making money tough to talk about in the church.

Topics left unspoken breed suspicion, so I'll remain completely open about what God's Word says so we can cast out the dark with the light of Truth.

In these perilous times, God is calling you to make a choice: Make the choice to reject Satan's worn-out old lies and decide today to put God first. That starts with obedience to the tithe.

I've included this helpful practical application guide to help you identify the subtle manipulations Satan has mastered. This is only to help you and never to harm or manipulate you into guilt giving.

Practical Application: Exposing Satan's Lies About Your Money

Lie Detection Worksheet

For each of Satan's lies below, understand the biblical truth that counteracts it:

1.   LIE: "God just wants your money."

TRUTH: God owns everything and doesn't need your money (Psalm 24:1). He wants your heart and trust, with tithing as evidence.

2. LIE: "You can't afford to tithe right now."

TRUTH: You can't afford not to tithe. God promises to bless obedience and rebuke the devourer (Malachi 3:10–11).

3. LIE: "Tithing was only for the Old Testament."

TRUTH: Tithing predates the law (Abraham, Genesis 14:20) and was affirmed by Jesus (Matthew 23:23).

4. LIE: "You should wait until you're more financially stable."

TRUTH: Stability comes through obedience, not before it. God meets needs when we put Him first (Matthew 6:33).

5. LIE: "Your church doesn't deserve your money."

TRUTH: The tithe isn't given to the church but to God. It's about your heart, not the worthiness of recipients.

Blessing Inventory

Journal ten ways God has already provided for you and your family:

Prayer of Declaration

Read aloud: "I declare that Satan's lies about money and tithing have no power over me. I choose to believe God's Word over my fears. I break agreement with the spirit of mammon and choose God as my provider.

My money will not be my master. I trust God to meet all my needs according to His riches in glory. In Jesus' name, Amen."

CHAPTER SUMMARY: **The Four Key Takeaways**

1.**Satan's Primary Strategy**—The enemy uses money as a wedge to separate us from God, just as he used fruit in the garden of Eden.

2.**The Mammon Spirit**—We cannot serve both God and mammon; tithing is a direct rejection of mammon's claim on our lives.

3.**Financial Revelation**—Our bank statements reveal our true priorities and who we truly serve.

4.**Breaking Deception**—Identifying and rejecting Satan's lies about tithing opens the door to God's blessing. We go through that door in obedience and by faith.

SECTION TWO:
OVERCOMING RESISTANCE

CHAPTER 4

FAITH OVER FEAR:
THE ROLE OF TRUST
IN GOD'S PROVISION

HEART CHECK

I TRUST the Chapter 3's assignment of examining your bank account register of expenses was revealing. How much or how little, if at all, you tithe and give is strictly between you and the Lord.

I do pray if you had to search high and low to find the last time a little something was tossed in the basket, that Holy Spirit assured you God loves you.

The Lord also wants you to commit to moving into a right posture of honoring Him with your wealth and your words. It's impossible to see Satan's lies while you are still being blinded by them.

REFLECTION QUESTION: What emotions surfaced as you examined your bank statements? What might God be revealing to you through those feelings?

THE NEXT CHALLENGE I asked the church was if they felt uneasy when I first mentioned the tithe. You've given ample time to reading this book if you've come this far, so great going and thank you.

What was your first reaction when you saw the focus for honoring God through obedience was the tithe? Have you ever stopped to wonder why you have such a deep-seated emotional connection to money?

I'm sorry to break this to you, but money has no emotion —it doesn't love you back, and it won't even say goodbye when it's gone.

So why do we hold on so tightly?

Fear.

The Fear Factor: What's Really Behind Our Resistance

Is your fear about not having enough money, or not trusting God enough to provide? It's a very real question and your willingness to press into a true answer will be incredibly helpful in guiding you away from worshipping mammon and instead, depending on God the Father. This fear keeps you in a poverty mindset where Satan wants you trapped, while hindering your relationship with God.

The Psychology of Financial Fear

Our relationship with money is complex and often shaped by childhood experiences, cultural messages, and past financial traumas. Research shows that financial decisions are frequently driven by emotion rather than logic. Consider these common fear-based responses to tithing:

1. Scarcity Mindset

Many people operate from a belief that there's never enough. This scarcity thinking contradicts God's promise of abundance and provision.

When we believe resources are limited, we clutch tightly to what we have rather than giving generously and living open-handed. Here are a few of my go-to Scriptures: Matthew 6:3 and 2 Peter 1:3.

2. Security Idol

For many, money represents safety and security. Tithing feels like removing a brick from our wall of protection. Yet Scripture teaches that true security comes from God alone, not our bank accounts. Here are a few of my go-to Scriptures: Proverbs 3:26 and Psalm 91:2.

3. Control Illusion

Holding on to money gives us a sense of control in an unpredictable world. Tithing requires surrendering control to God—admitting He knows better how to direct our resources. Here is one of my go-to Scriptures: Matthew 6:25–33.

4. Past Pain Projection

Previous financial hardships create fear of future lack. If you've experienced poverty or financial crisis, tithing can trigger anxiety about returning to that state.

God invites us to trust His future provision rather than projecting past pain (2 Timothy 1:7).

SATAN HOLDS the key to the chain of fear, but truth of the Word is the bolt cutter that sets you free. We always find ourselves in conflict over cash, but money isn't the problem —the love of money is the problem:

"For the love of money is a root of all kinds of evil, for which some have strayed from the faith in their greediness and pierced themselves through with many sorrows" (1 Timothy 6:10 NKJV).

This is worth repeating: God wants you to have money— God Does Not want money to have you.

Scientific Research on Generosity and Wellbeing

Modern research has uncovered fascinating connections between generosity and human flourishing that align perfectly with biblical principles of giving:

Neurological Benefits

Studies using functional MRI technology show that generosity activates the brain's reward centers, releasing hormones like dopamine, serotonin, and oxytocin—the same "feel good" chemicals released during other pleasurable activities. When we give, our brains literally light up with pleasure.

Physical Health Improvements

Research published in the *Journal of Health Psychology* found that regular givers experience:

• Lower blood pressure
• Reduced stress levels
• Strengthened immune systems

•Longer lifespans (up to five years longer in some studies)

Mental Health Benefits

Multiple studies have documented that consistent givers report:

•Reduced rates of depression

•Lower anxiety levels

•Greater life satisfaction

•Enhanced sense of purpose and meaning

Relational Strengthening

Generous people typically experience:

•Stronger community connections

•More meaningful relationships

•Greater trust from others

•Expanded social networks

This research confirms what Scripture has taught for thousands of years: "It is more blessed to give than to receive" (Acts 20:35). The design of generosity into our very biology is proof that we were created to be givers, not hoarders.

RESEARCH INSIGHT: A 2017 study by the University of Zurich, titled "<u>A Neural Link Between Generosity and Happiness</u>," found that even the intention to be generous triggers neural changes that increase happiness.

Participants who merely committed to generosity (before giving anything) showed greater happiness than those who planned to spend on themselves.

THIS PRINCIPLE of trusting God despite fear isn't just theoretical—I've seen it transform lives. Sarah is one such person who agreed to share her journey. Of course, I've changed her name and anything that might make her identifiable, not because she's entering the witness protection program, but Five Stones is a family church, and I value her privacy.

The testimonies I share were written by the people who lived them. Sarah called hers "Finding Provision in the Valley."

Finding Provision in the Valley: Sarah's Testimony

I remember clutching the "final notice" in my hands as they trembled. As a single mother of two young boys, I was already stretching every dollar to its breaking point.

The divorce had left me with mountains of debt, and child support payments were inconsistent at best.

I'd been attending church for years but always skipped past the sermons on tithing. I still cry when I think about the struggle and embarrassment that caused me. How could God possibly expect me to give the first 10 percent when I couldn't even make ends meet?

My turning point came during a particularly difficult month when my hours were cut at work.

I was terrified, I admit. But something in me just knew—I needed to trust God completely. I calculated my tithe from my reduced hours paycheck—$37.40—and it felt like giving away groceries for the week.

What happened next wasn't an instant miracle. There was no mysterious envelope of cash or surprise inheritance. Instead, I experienced something more sustainable.

Within two weeks, a neighbor offered to watch my boys after school, saving me $160 in monthly childcare costs. Then my supervisor created a new position with more stable hours specifically for me.

Three years later, I not only continue to tithe but I'm also debt free.

The most unexpected blessing wasn't financial, I learned. It was the peace I found in the middle of my circumstances. For the first time, I wasn't facing life as a single mom alone—I was in partnership with God as my provider.

REFLECTION QUESTION: What specific fear is holding you back from tithing faithfully? Name it specifically, then counteract it with God's promise from Scripture.

When Did Scripture Expire?

Sarah's faith was not based on some new scheme or technology. It was grounded in the eternal Word of God. Christian comfort and convenience have made an art form out of cherry-picking which parts of the Bible best suit their current situation. Sections of God's eternal Word are treated like expired milk in the refrigerator.

Christians have been seduced into thinking that tithing is outdated and something only tied to the Old Testament and

Mosaic law. We can't blame resistance to tithing entirely on Satan.

Many churches teach that tithing is obsolete, and many Christians have adopted this position. Simple question asked once again, "When did God abolish the law?"

Jesus made this clear:

"Don't misunderstand why I have come. I did not come to abolish the law of Moses or the writings of the prophets. No, I came to accomplish their purpose.

I tell you the truth, until heaven and earth disappear, not even the smallest detail of God's law will disappear until its purpose is achieved" (Matthew 5:17–18 NLT).

The Continuity of Scripture: Old and New Testament in Harmony

It deeply grieves me to see people who claim to love God, but openly dishonor Him by either rejecting His Word, remaining ignorant of what Scripture says, or flat out rebelling against truth.

I'll admit that there are many mysteries planted within the Bible that have yet to be revealed, but Matthew 5:17–18 is not one of them. It's crystal clear, and for the Old Testament disregarders, let's look at evidence, not emotion.

The Purpose of the Law

Matthew 5:17:—"...I came to accomplish their purpose."

What was the purpose of the law and writings of the prophets?

1.To reveal God's character.

2.To expose our sin.

3.To direct us to Christ for salvation.

The Duration of the Law

Matthew 5:18:—"...until heaven and earth disappear..."

Jesus gave a new law, which did not abolish the old, but fulfilled it. Jesus was saying that the law cannot be changed. It will only end when our current world system ends as heaven and earth disappear and... When will that be?

"Then I, John, saw the holy city, New Jerusalem, coming down out of heaven from God, prepared as a bride adorned for her husband" (Revelation 21:2 NKJV).

The Scope of the Law

Matthew 5:18: "Not even the smallest detail of God's law will disappear until its purpose is achieved."

What are those purposes?

•Lead us into relationship with God.

•Point us to Jesus.

The Relationship Between Law and Grace

Here's where many Christians misunderstand the relationship between the Old and New Testaments. The New Testament doesn't abolish the principles of the Old; it fulfills and transforms them through Christ. Consider these key distinctions:

1. Condemnation vs. Empowerment

Under the Old Covenant, the law condemned us by exposing our inability to meet God's standard. Under the

New Covenant, the Holy Spirit empowers us to fulfill the heart of the law through relationship with Christ.

2. External Compliance vs. Internal Transformation

The Old Covenant focused on external compliance with rules. The New Covenant transforms us from within, writing God's laws on our hearts (Jeremiah 31:33).

3. Fear vs. Love

The Old Covenant often motivated through fear of punishment. The New Covenant motivates through love and gratitude for what Christ has done.

4. Shadow vs. Substance

The Old Testament practices were shadows pointing to Christ (Colossians 2:17). In Christ, we have the substance to which those shadows pointed.

No wonder Satan wants you to ignore the Old Testament!!!!

As a believer, you are not under the law's curse of condemnation, but you cannot steal, murder, rape, lie, or commit adultery. Tithing is not a matter of Old Testament versus New Testament or law versus grace. It is about relationship.

Exposing Satan's Greatest Deception About God

While we are batting down bad beliefs, let's expose another one of Satan's deceptions. Have you ever heard, or better yet, said, "God just wants your money!"

The truth is, God owns everything—He doesn't need your money.

"The earth is the Lord's, and all its fullness,

The world and those who dwell therein" (Psalm 24:1 NKJV).

The moment you stop buying into the lies and embrace the truth, you'll enjoy the blessings that God desires to give you, and the power to acquire wealth to show He is your covenant provider. I shared this Scripture earlier, but it is worth restating here.

"And you shall remember the Lord your God, for it is He who gives you power to get wealth, that He may establish His covenant which He swore to your fathers, as it is this day" (Deuteronomy 8:18 NKJV).

And for those who favor the New Testament, consider this:

"And God will generously provide all you need. Then you will always have everything you need, and plenty left over to share with others" (2 Corinthians 9:8 NLT).

Does that sound like, "God just wants your money!"?

God's Desire for Covenant Relationship

Provision is part of God's character and in that character, God desires relationship with you. So, what does relationship with God look like? That's a great question. Too often we hold relationships as casual acquaintances or friends, but God moves within an eternal realm.

We use terms like BFF (best friends forever), but we have no concept of forever. Only God is the eternal God of forever. Covenant relationships reflect His nature and one way He establishes that partnership with you is through wealth provisions.

God's principle of first giving is an example to lost people that His covenant of redemption remains active. Instead of openly receiving from God, we argue about His intentions and ability to provide even while we live within the realm of all that He has provided.

Romans 12:2 tells us that we must not copy the behavior and customs of this world, but let God transform us into a new person by changing the way we think. Only then we will know God's will for us, which is good and pleasing and perfect.

We must renew our relational minds in the way we approach those relationships. We cannot ascribe to God the qualities of how we treat each other. Nor can we define how we expect Him to treat us.

We usually think of wealth and provisions as something we must earn on our own. It gives us a sense of pride, influence, and identity, but do you see the problems with that?

God looks at provision differently. He sees it as a good Father caring for His covenant family. We must renew our minds in the way we think of God's provisions.

We resent the "Joneses" because the world says we must "keep up" with them. God says He blessed the Joneses as an example of how He loves and provides for them. God shows His covenant through provision.

Will God provide for you? Yes.

Has God always provided for you? Yes

He provided His only Son for your life; do you think He will withhold what you need to thrive?

"For God so loved the world that He gave His only begotten Son, that whoever believes in Him should not perish but have everlasting life" (John 3:16 NKJV).

I pray you will take a moment and allow this to resonate with you. The Father gave His only Son as a ransom (1 Timothy 2:6) because you handed the keys to every perfect thing God created over to Satan.

The same one that has fed you lies about the tithes had you on the H-E-double L express. If not for the abundant generosity of our good Father, this life would be doomed to eternal damnation.

Would you give your child for people who reject you? If as a Christian you refuse to honor God by giving the tithe, then you could never imagine the love it took for Him to give His Son.

No, God doesn't want your money; He wants your heart.

Chapter Summary: The Four Key Takeaways

1.Fear Masquerades as Theological Objection—Our resistance to tithing is often rooted in fear, not biblical understanding.

2.Scripture Maintains Its Authority—Jesus didn't abolish the law but fulfilled it; biblical principles remain in effect today.

3.Science Confirms Scripture—Modern research reveals the neurological, physical, and psychological benefits of generosity that Scripture has taught for millennia.

4.God Wants Relationship, Not Resources—The ultimate purpose of tithing is to deepen our covenant connection with God, not to fund religious institutions.

CHAPTER 5

THE PRINCIPLE OF FIRST: HONORING GOD FOR LASTING IMPACT

FEELINGS ARE NOT FACTS

HAVE you ever wondered why our expectations of blessings seem tied to our emotions? The truth is God's blessings flow from one unchanging principle: obedience.

While we may feel uncertain, unworthy, or entitled, God's kingdom operates through His order, structure, and authority. Obedience is the key to unlocking His abundant blessings, not your feelings.

The Principle of First: God's Eternal Design

Throughout Scripture, we see a consistent pattern—God always asks for the first and best. This principle appears in multiple forms:

I. Firstfruits in Agricultural Societies

In ancient Israel's agricultural economy, God commanded His people to bring the first and best of their harvest (Exodus 23:19). This wasn't about the quantity but about the priority—acknowledging God's provision before enjoying it themselves.

2. Firstborn Dedication

God claimed all firstborn sons and animals (Exodus 13:2), instituting a redemption system that foreshadowed Christ's ultimate redemptive work. This principle established that the first belongs to God.

3. First Hours of the Day

The pattern of morning prayer throughout Scripture (Psalm 5:3, Mark 1:35) establishes that our first waking moments belong to God.

4. First Day of the Week

The Sabbath principle (and later Sunday worship for Christians) set aside the first day as holy to the Lord, establishing the pattern for the rest of the week.

The principle of first is more than a religious ritual—it's a divine pattern woven into creation itself. When we honor God with our first and best in any area, He establishes a pattern of blessing for what follows.

This is why God's challenge in Malachi remains relevant —He wants to demonstrate His faithfulness through our obedience.

Obedience is an ongoing commitment to honor God's commands. One area where this principle is crucial is in our finances. God calls us to demonstrate obedience through tithing—a practice that reflects our trust in His provision.

PEOPLE TRY PLACING the Almighty God in a predefined box or treat Jesus like a genie in a bottle. They expect their wishes to come true if they just close their eyes hard enough or squeeze their hands tight and hope for good karma because they feel like they are a good person.

That's not how God's kingdom principles work. God doesn't want your hopeful wishes. He wants your heart. That starts with your obedience.

The Simplicity of Tithing: Understanding the Basic Command

I understand most things at the core level. When I read God's Word, I trust it is true. What is your first thought when you read Malachi 3:10—"Bring all the tithes into the storehouse?"

I'm thinking what God says, He means. A tithe is a tenth. That's the actual definition of the word and it literally means one-tenth or 10 percent. God won't bless you as much as He wants to bless you if you withhold part of the tithe.

God is not a used car dealer you can haggle with on percentage points. He established the tenth as a standard of blessing, not a burden to bear.

So, keeping it simple, I'm bringing my whole tithe to the storehouse. The storehouse is the local church where you are fed. If you attend a church and you are not being fed the meat of God's gospel message, I'd suggest you not return to that church. Immediately find yourself a Holy Spirit-filled, Bible-teaching church that teaches the meat of God's Word.

Once you obey God's first command to bring your whole tithe as an offering, you can move freely through the rest of His promise. This is the only place in Scripture where God invites you to test Him.

If you have yet to experience God's tangible, flowing river of blessings in your life, it might be because you've yet to move into the position to receive it. Where do you find that spot? It's located at obedience.

Modern Applications of the Storehouse Principle

The concept of the "storehouse" has evolved as society has changed, but the principle remains consistent. Let's explore what this means in today's context:

What Is the Modern Storehouse?

In Malachi's day, the storehouse was the temple treasury where tithes were collected to support priests, maintain the temple, and care for the poor. Today, the principle applies to the local church where you receive spiritual nourishment.

Digital Economy Considerations

Our modern economy introduces new questions about tithing:

•**Multiple Income Streams:** Many people have various income sources beyond traditional employment. The principle applies to all increase.

•**Non-monetary Assets:** Stock options, cryptocurrency, and other non-cash assets are still increase that falls under the tithing principle.

• TIMING OF TITHING: In a world of automatic deposits and online banking, we can schedule tithing to truly be our first financial priority.

Special Circumstances

• **When Traveling:** Some wonder about tithing while away from their home church. The principle is about honoring God first, not about geographical location.

• **Between Churches:** During transitions between churches, the tithe can be set aside for later giving until you find your new spiritual home.

• **Missions Support:** Some feel called to support mission work directly. While commendable, this is giving beyond the tithe, not a replacement for it.

PRACTICAL TIP: Set up automatic transfers that move your tithe to a separate account immediately when you're paid. This helps establish the "first" principle in practice and removes the temptation to spend what belongs to God. Then, after you have prayed over it and blessed your tithe, break it from your control as you tithe to the Lord.

The principle of putting God first isn't just for those who are financially comfortable. Let me share how one young professional discovered the power of this truth even while facing significant student debt.

Remember, I've asked each person to write out their testimony along with talking with me about it. This young man we'll call Marcus shared what he called, "Breaking the Career Ceiling."

Breaking the Career Ceiling: Marcus's Testimony

Fresh out of college with $67,000 in student loan debt, I landed my first professional job in marketing with a starting salary of $48,000.

My college pastor had taught about tithing, but I had always assumed it was something to start "someday" when I was financially stable.

I had my five-year plan all mapped out, I justified. Pay down debt aggressively for three years, then start building savings, then maybe consider tithing once I hit the $75K salary mark.

During a church tithing sermon, I calculated what my tithe would be—$400 monthly—and immediately dismissed it as impossible given my debt obligations and the high cost of living in the DFW metro area.

But I couldn't shake this nagging feeling that I was approaching my entire financial life backward. I confessed. I was building my future on my own ability rather than God's provision.

I decided to take God up on His test for six months. I automatically transferred the tithe with each paycheck before paying any other bills. I chose to auto draft because I wanted to eliminate any temptation to stop.

The adjustment required practical changes—moving to a shared apartment, meal prepping instead of eating out for most meals, and delaying some purchases—most vanity items.

The tangible results weren't immediate, but they were significant, I admit. Within my first year of tithing, I received two unexpected promotions that increased my salary by 22 percent. But more importantly, I experienced a profound shift in how I viewed money and success altogether.

Today, four years later, I have eliminated my student debt, continue to faithfully tithe, and now I mentor other young professionals in biblical financial principles.

What I didn't expect was how tithing would transform my career ambitions. I'm no longer climbing the ladder just for myself. My definition of success completely changed when I put God first in my finances.

Still Relevant Today: Tithing's Origin Story

Everyone who has shared their testimony like Marcus explains that an understanding of Scripture unlocked their hearts to honor God through obedience to the tithe as the starting point of deep relationship.

I've mentioned it earlier, but because it's so foundational, I want to touch base on the origin story of the tithe once again. My concern is rooted in what I hear when speaking with Christians who struggle with not just finances, but relationships.

They repeat things they've heard about the law as if it's a dirty word. I always caution people in these conversations to truly think through their intentions.

Scripture is not some piece of federal government legislation you oppose. The entirety of the Bible represents

God's holy Word. Yes, even the "law." Shredding God's Word with emotional scissors can lead you further into a path called rebellion.

Deuteronomy 4:2 clearly warns against this: "You shall not add to the word which I command you, nor take from it, that you may keep the commandments of the Lord your God which I command you" (NKJV).

Additionally, Deuteronomy 12:32, Proverbs 30:5–6 and Revelation 22:18–19 affirm this. Obedience is sometimes measured in your opposition to the action yet honoring it because you love God.

People who are either confused about what Scripture says, who have been manipulated by prosperity pastors, or who are in willful rebellion, declare that they are free from the tithe because it was mandated in the Mosaic law. Thanks to Jesus Christ we are indeed covered by grace, but we are not free from the law.

It bears repeating, but we are still under the sections of the law that were strengthened in the new covenant because Jesus did not abolish the law (Matthew 5:17–18).

When He fulfilled the law, we were saved by grace from the condemnation of the law. With all that being said, the tithe did not originate with the law. God's tithe predates the Mosaic law by over four hundred and thirty years.

The Pre-Law Foundation of Tithing

Abraham, of whom we are all spiritual descendants (Romans 4:16) established the standard of tithing to God when he gave a tenth to Melchizedek, priest of God most high—the forerunner to Jesus Christ.

"Then Melchizedek king of Salem brought out bread and wine; he was the priest of God Most High. And he blessed him and said:

'Blessed be Abram of God Most High,

Possessor of heaven and earth;

And blessed be God Most High,

Who has delivered your enemies into your hand.'

And he gave him a tithe of all (Genesis 14:18–20 NKJV).

The Melchizedek Connection to Christ

The connection between Abraham's tithe to Melchizedek and our relationship to Christ is profound. Hebrews 7 elaborates on this connection, showing that Melchizedek was a type of Christ—"without father, without mother, without genealogy, having neither beginning of days nor end of life, but made like the Son of God" (Hebrews 7:3 NKJV).

When Abraham tithed to Melchizedek, he was acknowledging a priesthood greater than the later Levitical priesthood. Christ is "a priest forever according to the order of Melchizedek" (Hebrews 7:17), meaning the principles established in this encounter—including tithing—continue under Christ's eternal priesthood.

If that's not good enough to convince the "It's the law" crowd, Abraham's grandson Jacob also tithed. About four hundred years before the law, Jacob (Israel) gave a tithe to the Lord.

"Then Jacob made a vow, saying, 'If God will be with me, and keep me in this way that I am going, and give me bread to eat and clothing to put on, so that I come back to my father's house in peace, then the Lord shall be my God. And this stone which I have set as a pillar shall be God's house, and of all that You give me I will surely give a tenth to You.'" (Genesis 28:20–22 NKJV).

The Vow:

I'd like you to notice what Scripture says about the tithe Jacob brought before the Lord. He made a vow, which is the continuation of an action with no end. Jacob's tithe to God was a vow, and just like marriage vows, it remains a lifelong commitment to honor the Lord.

Tithing, just like your salvation, is not based on the rise and fall of human emotions or opinions. Once you commit to faithful tithing, God has already proven through word and deeds what He will do for you. God's promise of abundant blessing (Malachi 3:10) follows our faithful obedience.

Tithing vs. Giving: Understanding the Distinction

Since we are dealing in facts and not feelings, let's address one more thing before moving forward. "Giving cheerfully" (2 Corinthians 9:7) has become the counter-tithe argument among many well-intentioned Christians. It's the New Testament chic for back-patting and tithe avoiding.

I completely get that. Leah and I were at that place while we battled against the legitimacy of the tithe. What we were battling was bad teaching and false doctrines of man designed to manipulate us into dishing out our earnings instead of honoring God with our obedience to tithe.

We'd high-five each other because we always gave at least 30 percent no matter what our income looked like. We had years of making seven figures and years of making, well, a whole lot less. Either way, we always gave generously. Except we refused to tithe.

Now, you might reason that within our 30 percent, the first 10 percent was counted as our tithe, but God's kingdom principles do not work like that.

It would be as illegitimate as driving sixty miles per hour in a thirty mile per hour zone and explaining to the police officer that the legal limit of thirty was met, so it makes everything above legit. Bad intentions do not make for good giving.

Tithing: The Foundation of Financial Obedience

The tithe (10 percent) is:

•**Mandatory**—A command, not a suggestion, and established before the law.

•**Fixed**—Always 10 percent of increase.

•**First**—Given before other expenses.

•**Focused**—Directed to the storehouse (local church).

•**Foundational**—The starting point of financial obedience.

GIVING: The Expression of Financial Generosity

Giving (beyond the tithe) is:

• **Voluntary**—According to personal decision.

• **Variable**—Amount determined by the giver.

• **Flexible**—Given as opportunities arise.

• **Free**—Can be directed to various needs.

• **Flowing**—Emerges from a generous heart.

Because we rejected the tithe, we also failed to consecrate (set apart) our first offering to the Lord as we are told in Exodus 23:19, " As you harvest your crops, bring the very best of the first harvest to the house of the Lord your God" (NLT). We continue to limit the potential for abundant peace and provision.

It is that act of transitioning your money into a supernatural transference that opens your authority to declare blessings and redemption for the rest of your money.

Thank God we were delivered by the truth of His Word through Scripture. One of the freedoms in that truth revealed was that indeed we are free to give generously, but in accordance with kingdom structure, we first honored the Lord by setting apart the tithe.

We also learned through Scripture that you do not pay tithes. You cannot pay to God what is already His. You bring it before the Lord.

The tithe represents our trust and obedience. While tithing demonstrates obedience, giving and offerings allow us to express love and gratitude to God. Both are valuable but distinct ways of honoring Him.

Another mistake people make is declaring they do not tithe because New Testament Scripture gave them the freedom to give as they feel. That is wrong. By rejecting the tithe, you reject God's redemption of the consecrated firstfruit offering. We've seen what that looks like in Malachi, when the Lord says He will rebuke the devourer.

"'And I will rebuke the devourer for your sakes,
So that he will not destroy the fruit of your ground,
Nor shall the vine fail to bear fruit for you in the field,'
Says the Lord of hosts" (Malachi 3:11 NKJV).

The Devourer: Understanding What Consumes Your Resources

Ever wonder where your money goes in between paychecks? It goes to the devourer. Misspending, wasteful expenditures, gambling, poor stewardship, vices, hobbies, addictions, bad habits, just to name a few. I will admit that the devourer, who God promises to rebuke, had, at times, his way with our earnings.

The devourer is anything that consumes your provisions outside of healthy stewardship. We all waste money on things like unused subscriptions, unvisited gym memberships, ordering food delivery instead of preparing meals and so on.

National data shows the average American wastes eighteen thousand dollars per year on illegitimate and unintended expenses. When you are the "god" over your gold, Satan is your banker, not you.

Only when you honor God with your firstfruits offering, the tithe, will He redeem the other 90 percent of your money.

Common Devourers in Modern Life

1. Impulse Purchases

The average American spends $324 per month on impulse buys—nearly $4,000 annually. These unplanned purchases often bring temporary satisfaction but lasting financial strain.

2. Subscription Services

Many people pay for multiple streaming services, apps, and memberships they rarely use. The average household wastes $348 annually on unused subscriptions they've forgotten about.

3. Food Waste

Americans throw away approximately 30 percent of the food they purchase, equivalent to about $1,500 per household annually.

4. Convenience Fees

ATM fees, rush shipping, delivery surcharges, and other convenience costs add up to an average of $2,400 per year for many families.

The Generosity Shift

5. Interest Payments

The average American household carries $6,270 in credit card debt, often paying 18–25 percent interest—resulting in thousands of dollars going to interest payments annually.

6. Emotional Spending

Using shopping as therapy leads to purchases that bring momentary happiness but long-term financial stress. This can consume 10–15 percent of take-home pay for many people.

God's promise to "rebuke the devourer" isn't just spiritual—it's eminently practical. When we honor God with our firstfruits, He helps us identify and eliminate wasteful spending, multiplying the effectiveness of the remaining 90 percent.

What you choose to do with the reminder of what God has given you is your choice. This is where the giving comes from, not before the tithe or in place of the tithe. They are very different opportunities to encounter relationship with God. Take a quick look at this Scripture:

Cheerful Giver:

"He who sows sparingly will also reap sparingly, and he who sows bountifully will also reap bountifully. So let each one give as he purposes in his heart, not grudgingly or of necessity; for God loves a cheerful giver" (2 Corinthians 9:6–7 NKJV).

This is a favorite for people who claim God ended tithing or allows them to give if they feel like it. We must not

67

manipulate Holy Scripture to accommodate our personal opinions. This Scripture is not about the tithe. It is about giving.

We know this because it plainly says, "give." If it were about the tithe, there would be no variable of what is sowed or what is reaped. It would read: He who sows 10 percent will reap 10 percent.

There is a difference in the ratio of what you reap because it is based on what you sow. Tithing has no variable. It is always 10 percent because the word "tithe" means tenth.

It's natural to have strong feelings about finances, especially around giving. But God's Word invites us to look beyond our emotions and seek truth in His promises.

Rather than focusing on verses that may seem to validate our comfort zones, we're called to trust the Scripture, understanding that God's principles are for our good and His glory.

Do you love your spouse and family only when you feel like it? Remember, this is about relationship.

Let's round out this chapter with a fact. Why does God require your tithe? Because it takes faith. Faith in God. Not faith in mammon. If it were easy, it would not hold value in making sure God was your priority.

Leah and I have been there, and we understand. If this feels hard, know that God honors your honesty. If you trust God—He will give you the courage to honor Him through

His Word. He will also bless you abundantly for allowing Him to show Himself to you.

Practical Application: Calculate Your Tithe

Take a pause from reading to reflect on your relationship with tithing and giving. What thoughts or emotions arise when you consider giving a full tithe? Do you feel hesitant, unsure, or inspired to obey God?

Take a moment to invite God into these thoughts, asking Him to help you see tithing as a way to grow closer to Him and experience His provision through trust and faith.

I'm going to share a quick practical application at this point in hopes you are truly interested in knowing exactly what your tithe should be. I shared this with our church in the first week, and I've included those instructions for you by pasting them straight from my sermon notes:

HOW TO KNOW WHAT TO BRING BEFORE GOD?

Great question—let's keep it super practical.

Take out your phone and go to the calculator app.

Type in the gross income amount you get paid—some are paid daily, weekly, twice a month, monthly—it works no matter your pay schedule.

Enter that amount in the app

Hit the X—multiplication sign.

That's a great sign because this is what God wants to do —multiply your provisions.

Type in .10

Now hit the Equal sign.

The amount on your screen is God's portion—your Tithe.

That is the key to unlocking God's kingdom provisions.

NOTE: Screenshot your calculator screen.

Save it in your pics throughout this series.

If you already tithe that amount, Amen.

Pray about being more generous and more blessed through giving above the tithe.

If that amount causes you to struggle to tithe, let it be an example of how far you are from having full faith in God to provide abundantly for you.

Also, pray about what is so important about that dollar amount that keeps you from trusting God more than money.

Finally, pray that God frees you from the slavery to that dollar amount so He can bless you much more abundantly than what your phone app shows.

Keep that screenshot as you move through the book and expect God to speak to you about how He loves you and wants to bless you abundantly.

Transforming Currency into Covenant: The Consecration Process

I also want to bless you with a real example of what our time of worship looks like at church. I've pasted the tithing notes below for reference, but the key is we attach everything to Scripture, and we do not ask for tithes to be brought before the Lord until they have been properly set apart and consecrated. I do not want anyone to miss the

blessings of God because the church failed to teach
them how.

Scripture:

*"Then Isaac sowed in that land and reaped in the same year a
hundredfold; and the Lord blessed him (Genesis 26:12 NKJV).*

HOLD ON BEFORE YOU BRING YOUR TITHES:

*Before you honor the Lord with your Firstfruits by the tithe—
I want you to apply God's principle to it and be Blessed.*

*Start learning to turn the monetary amount into a holy
offering.*

*When you set it apart—it is no longer money—it is a holy,
consecrated offering before God.*

Stop thinking about it as a dollar amount—*Start praying
Blessings, Abundance and Multiplication into it as your holy,
consecrated, set apart offering to God.*

*Once YOU make that supernatural shift, YOU can start
praying your blessings over the OFFERING—Not the dollar
amount.*

God MULTIPLIES your offering, not your MONEY.

*And when you bring your tithes and offerings before the Lord
—it is no longer money—it is God's offering to multiply.*

Just like Jesus did for the loaves and fishes.

*Sowing into God's kingdom activates a supernatural release of
His abundant blessings.*

I encourage you to start applying God's instructions on
how to treat His tithe so that you realize an abundant
blessing through your obedience to the Lord.

Chapter Summary: The Four Key Takeaways

1.The Principle of First Is God's Eternal Design—
Throughout Scripture, God consistently asks for our first and best as a pattern of priority and honor.

2.Tithing Predates the Law—Abraham's and Jacob's examples show that tithing was established as a principle of faith centuries before the Mosaic law.

3.Tithing and Giving Are Distinct—The tithe is the required first 10 percent, while offerings represent giving beyond the tithe from a cheerful heart.

4.Consecration Transforms Currency—When we set apart our tithe as holy, it becomes more than money—it becomes a sacred covenant connection with God.

PRACTICAL WORKSHEET: Creating Your Tithing Budget

Monthly Income: $_____

Tithe (10%): $_____

Essential Expenses:

—Housing (25%): $_____

—Transportation (15%): $_____

—Food (10%): $_____

—Savings (10%): $_____

Remaining for other expenses: $_____

CHAPTER 6

THE PRINCIPLE OF FIRST
— GIVING THAT LASTS

THE TITHING PATHWAY
TO RELATIONSHIP

ONE GLORIOUS SATURDAY morning during a men's breakfast for the church, I was asked a few questions about the tithe. I used the analogy that the tithe is like a pulling guard in football.

He creates a path for the running back by clearing the opposing team's tacklers. The tithe clears the heart's path to relationship with God.

In a world filled with distractions competing for our attention, God has given us a powerful resource to keep our focus on Him: the Principle of First. God gave us His first and best in His Son, Jesus.

This offering for the sins of the world redeemed us into a state of righteousness before God. Giving His best is a part of God's character, and for us to reflect that same character, we are called to also offer up our first and best to God so He can redeem the rest of our provision.

This principle is about more than finances; it's a way of aligning our hearts with God's eternal priorities, reminding us that everything we have is His.

Through tithing, firstfruits, and giving, God calls us to put Him first, which leads to lasting blessings and an unshakeable relationship with Him. The Principle of First is the key to activating the will of God by aligning ourselves with that will.

"We love Him because He first loved us" (1 John 4:19 NKJV).

This matters because the chaos around us is meant to draw our attention away from God's peace. Tithing allows us to quiet that noise by setting our eyes on Him. It exposes areas where our hearts may resist surrender and gently brings them back to the Father.

As we prioritize God with the first part of our resources, we invite His peace and guidance to fill every part of our lives. Tithing is not about money. It's about relationship with God.

Beyond Religious Obligation: The Journey to Relational Giving

When Leah and I first encountered teaching on tithing, it was challenging. We'd been exposed to misinterpretations that turned tithing into an obligation but mostly a burden. Though we gave, our hearts were resistant to the concept of tithing.

But over time, through sound teaching, and personal study, we realized that God established the tithe to protect our hearts from materialism and keep us close to Him. The tithe wasn't about funding a 501c3 nonprofit organization; it was a way to safeguard our relationship with Him.

Religion vs. Relationship in Tithing

Many believers approach tithing from one of two problematic perspectives:

The Religious Approach

The religious approach to tithing is characterized by:

- Duty without delight
- External compliance without internal commitment
- Fear-based giving (to avoid punishment)
- Calculating the minimum required
- Focus on the rule rather than the relationship

This approach may maintain technical obedience but misses the heart of God's design for tithing.

The Relational Approach

The relational approach to tithing is characterized by:

- Delight in honoring God first
- Internal commitment that produces external actions
- Love-based giving (in response to God's generosity)
- Looking for opportunities to be generous beyond the minimum
- Focus on the relationship that the principle protects

This approach aligns with God's ultimate purpose for tithing—deepening our connection with Him.

If you're feeling challenged by this teaching, that's a good thing. It means you're seeking a deeper relationship with God. Scripture says in 2 Timothy 3:16, "All Scripture is given by inspiration of God, and is profitable for doctrine, for reproof, for correction, for instruction in righteousness" (NKJV).

God's Word is meant to stretch us so we can grow closer to Him. As we grow, we trust that He will never ask us to do something that would harm us.

Tithing is an act of obedience, but it's also a path to rest. Jesus says in Matthew 11:28–30, "Come to Me, all you who labor and are heavy laden, and I will give you rest... For My yoke is easy and My burden is light" (NKJV).

Tithing releases the burdens of materialism, fear, and pride, allowing us to rest in the assurance that God is our provider.

Breaking Soul Ties to Mammon

Part of that rest comes from the intentional act of breaking all soul ties that have you tethered to mammon (materialistic greed). Talking about money often brings up emotions of fear, greed, or shame. Satan has worked hard to attach these feelings to finances, making it harder for us to trust God with our resources.

UNDERSTANDING SOUL TIES **to Money**

In biblical understanding, a "soul tie" is a connection formed between our soul and something or someone else. While this concept is often discussed in the context of relationships, it applies powerfully to our connection with material possessions as well.

Money-related soul ties can form through:

•**Childhood experiences** where financial security was threatened

•**Traumatic financial events** like bankruptcy or job loss

•**Cultural messages** that equate worth with wealth

•**Family patterns** of financial fear or mismanagement

•**Prideful self-reliance** that rejects God's provision

These unhealthy connections create spiritual and emotional dependencies that prevent us from experiencing the freedom of trusting God with our finances.

Breaking Financial Soul Ties

Breaking unhealthy connections to money involves:

1.**Identification**—Recognizing the specific fears, attitudes, or patterns that have created unhealthy attachments to money

2.**Confession**—Acknowledging these attachments as contrary to God's design

3.**Renunciation**—Formally rejecting these connections through prayer

4.**Replacement**—Establishing new, healthy patterns based on biblical principles

5.Consecration—Dedicating your finances to God's purposes

If you've been hurt by past teachings that used tithing as a tool for manipulation, take a moment to release those hurts to God.

Forgive those who may have wronged you and break any soul ties to a materialistic mindset. God desires your heart above all, and when we tithe, we release money from having a hold over us.

Prayer for Breaking Financial Soul Ties

"Father, I recognize that I have formed unhealthy attachments to money through fear, pride, and past experiences. I confess that I have sometimes trusted in wealth more than in You.

I now renounce every soul tie to materialism and the spirit of mammon. I break agreement with financial fear and anxiety. I choose instead to trust You as my provider and to honor You with my firstfruits.

I consecrate my finances to Your purposes and ask that You establish new patterns of generosity and faith in my life. In Jesus' name, amen."

The best gift you can give yourself is forgiveness. Forgiveness frees you from the offense others have struck against you. You are free from the offense and the offender.

Once you step into that freedom, you will begin to expand your understanding of the heart of giving.

THE HEART OF FIRSTFRUITS: Setting Aside What's Holy

One of the most profound aspects of tithing is the way it clears our hearts and reorients us toward God. Tithing is not merely about finances; it is a direct route to aligning our values with God's eternal principles.

In James 1:18, we're reminded of our purpose as "firstfruits of His creatures," a calling that invites us to put God first in all things, setting aside what's His in faithfulness. This aligns our lives with His covenant and builds a deeper relationship with our Creator.

For many of us, tithing may carry memories of tension or discomfort. Some have been taught to see tithing as a duty or an obligation, leading to frustration rather than freedom.

But, as I've shared, even as mature believers, Leah and I had a season of misunderstanding around tithing, treating it as a burdensome "have-to."

Despite giving generously, we lacked peace around the practice because our understanding was incomplete. Once we learned the biblical principle behind it, our perspective changed, and so did the relationship with God. Growth in our faith often involves unlearning old ideas and replacing them with truth.

Part of that growth is also admitting that it can be challenging to tithe. But as we grow to know and love God, we come to trust that He never asks anything of us that would harm us. He calls us to follow His ways because they bring us rest and peace.

The Principle of Consecration: Setting Apart Our First for God

Part of this growth includes acknowledging the challenge of tithing. However, as we deepen our relationship with God, we come to understand that He only asks us to do things that are ultimately for our benefit of reflecting His character more clearly.

This is part of what I mentioned earlier about His yoke in Matthew 11:28–30. If your heart for God is anything other than easy and light, this chapter is the place for you to sit and meditate on what God is saying to you. His guidance brings us rest and peace.

In Exodus 13:2, God tells Israel to "Consecrate to Me all the firstborn...it is Mine." Consecration, from the Hebrew, "qadash," means "to set apart" or "to be holy." This practice of offering the first to God is more than an ancient ritual; it is an act of recognizing His rightful place in our lives.

Hebrew Insight: The Hebrew concept of "qadash" (consecration) carries the meaning of being set apart for a special purpose. When we consecrate our firstfruits to God, we're not just giving money—we're acknowledging that this portion is fundamentally different. It belongs to God in a way that's distinct from our other resources.

Proverbs 3:9–10 emphasizes this: "Honor the Lord with your possessions, and with the firstfruits of all your increase; so your barns will be filled with plenty." When we consecrate our first to God, He blesses the rest. (NKJV)

Tithing is about releasing control. By dedicating our first to God, we surrender our self-reliance and place our trust in His provision. In doing so, we allow God's blessing to touch every area of our lives.

Romans 11:16 explains that "if the firstfruit is holy, the lump is also holy" (NKJV), meaning that our firstfruits offering to God sanctifies the rest of our resources, opening them to His protection and provision. Tithing shields our finances and ensures that God's blessings flow abundantly in our lives.

The Three Dimensions of God's Blessing

Once you have consecrated your offering to God and prayed blessing over the tithe, God redeems the rest so you may enjoy the blessings of provision as you steward the remaining 90 percent. But, failing to honor Malachi 3:11 keeps the rest of your possessions vulnerable to mammon and wasted resources.

The devourer represents the forces that can lead us to stress over our finances, turning our attention away from God. Tithing sets us free from the idolization of money by anchoring our trust in God as our provider.

This freedom invites us to experience what Jesus promised in John 10:10b: "I have come that they may have life, and that they may have it more abundantly" (NKJV).

GOD'S BLESSINGS through tithing operate in three dimensions:

1. Material Blessing

While God doesn't promise wealth to all who tithe, He does promise provision. Many tithers testify to experiencing financial stability, debt reduction, and unexpected provision in tangible ways.

2. Spiritual Blessing

Tithing cultivates spiritual growth by developing trust, breaking materialism's hold, and aligning our hearts with God's priorities. This spiritual blessing often manifests as increased peace, joy, and discernment.

3. Relational Blessing

Perhaps the most significant dimension is the deepened relationship with God that comes through regular tithing. As we trust Him with our finances, we experience and understand His faithfulness in new ways.

None of these dimensions operates independently. They work together as a complete expression of God's desire to bless His children holistically—meeting needs in every dimension of life.

Practical Steps: Treating the Tithe as Sacred

1.Separate the Tithe First: When you receive income, take out the first 10 percent and set it aside as holy to God. This simple act declares that God is your priority, not just in word but in practice.

IF YOU GET PAID in cash or check, remove the tithe immediately and set it in an envelope. If you receive direct deposit, calculate God's 10 percent, pray a blessing over what you have consecrated and decide to transfer that amount online.

2.**Handle the Tithe with Reverence:** Tithing is not merely another transaction. Pray over your tithe, asking God to multiply its blessings and to use it for His Kingdom. Jesus demonstrated this principle in Mark 6:41 when He blessed the loaves and fish before distributing them, turning a small offering into a miracle that fed thousands. Pray that your offering will be used to bless others and grow God's work in your local church.

3.**Cultivate a Heart of Gratitude:** As you tithe, reflect on God's goodness and His provision. Tithing is an opportunity to express gratitude and trust, acknowledging that everything we have is ultimately from Him.

Your heart is what God wants. Growing a heart of gratitude through the tithe means you'll know God better than ever before.

Getting Practical About Your Tithing Practice

I want to add a little practical wisdom about getting practical. I cannot stress enough how much God loves you. I also can't stress enough that God wants to bless you, but there are kingdom principles that must be honored.

One of the biggest mistakes Christians make is feeling like they deserve something big from God and are disappointed if He fails to come through. Despite His gift of everlasting life being a pretty big deal, Christians tend to set unrealistic expectations on Him, yet they do not obey these simple principles.

I lived it and have witnessed countless others step into His abundant favor by simply getting practical about following the rules of His kingdom.

Even your hometown has laws and rules that you follow to avoid a ticket or a fine from an overzealous HOA, yet we act shocked that the Creator of this incredibly complex and beautifully structured universe has guidelines.

Modern Tithing in a Complex Financial World

Today's financial landscape presents unique challenges and opportunities for tithing that weren't relevant in biblical times:

Digital Tithing

•**Automatic Transfers:** Setting up recurring transfers that process immediately after your paycheck deposits ensures the firstfruits principle is honored.

•**Apps and Platforms:** Many churches now offer mobile giving options that make consistent tithing easier, especially for those who rarely carry cash.

Complex Income Sources

•**Investment Returns:** Tithing applies to all increase, including dividends, capital gains, and interest income.

•**Side Hustles:** Many believers have multiple income streams that should all be considered for tithing.

•**Irregular Income:** Commission-based workers and freelancers may need a systematic approach to ensure consistent tithing despite income fluctuations.

Special Financial Situations

•**Debt Repayment:** While working to become debt free, tithing helps align your priorities and may accelerate debt reduction through improved stewardship.

•**Retirement:** Fixed-income situations require wisdom, but the principle of honoring God first remains applicable.

•**Business Owners:** Calculating business income for tithing purposes may require professional counsel to determine appropriate "increase."

Allow me to offer a dose of loving tough love. Saying, "I can't afford to tithe!" is an emotional response to either fear or the love of money. The truth is you cannot afford to not tithe.

What in your daily temporary life is worth more than your eternal relationship with God? If you are willing to look at facts instead of feelings, you will see that you have more margin than you realize.

US Bureau of Labor shows that the 2024 average American weekly take-home paycheck is $1,143.00. Additionally, the average weekly spending for an individual is $554—housing, transportation, food, clothes, fun, etc.

A few quick calculator clicks:

Weekly Take-Home Pay—$1,143.00

Weekly Tithe—$1,14.30

Subtotal—$1,028.70

Weekly Average Expenses—$554.00

Weekly Discretionary Spending—$474.70

Deciding to tithe cannot be based on affordability. It is your personal invitation to trust God with your life. When we do, He promises to provide abundantly.

Tithes and offerings are expressions to assure the supernatural release of God's abundant blessing into your life. Our natural inclination is to work more to earn more, but that has a cap.

God's love and provision have no limits except the ones you set. You'll never go wrong, doing right in trusting God.

"Then Isaac sowed in that land and reaped in the same year a hundredfold; and the Lord blessed him" (Genesis 26:12 NKJV).

Can you imagine reaping 100 percent more? And that's not all, because in addition to one hundred times what Isaac sowed, the Lord blessed him. What are you sowing into your relationship with God?

Chapter Summary: The Four Key Takeaways

1.**Tithing Creates a Path to Relationship**—Like a pulling guard in football, tithing clears obstacles between us and deeper connection with God.

2.**Consecration Transforms Resources**—Setting apart your firstfruits helps you to break the grip on ordinary currency and begin to experience it as sowing seeds that invite God's supernatural multiplication.

3.God's Blessings Operate in Three Dimensions— Material, spiritual, and relational blessings flow from faithful tithing.

4.Practical Steps Make Tithing Sustainable—Modern financial tools and practices can help us implement biblical principles in today's complex economy.

SECTION THREE: IMPLEMENTING FAITHFUL GIVING

CHAPTER 7

WALKING IN FREEDOM: BREAKING MATERIALISM'S HOLD

WALKING IN THE FREEDOM OF GOD'S FAVOR

LET'S BE REAL—TITHING and putting God first in everything can feel like a challenge. Maybe you've thought, "Why can't I just give when I feel like it? Isn't that good enough?"

I've wrestled with those questions too. But here's the truth: God's blessings and favor come with an invitation to trust Him fully.

Before you start thinking, "Here we go, another catch," let me explain. God's principles aren't about taking something from you—they're about giving you something greater than what you have.

His invitation to live out the Principle of First is less about rules and more about relationship. It's not just about money either; it's about giving God your very best in every area of your life.

When Leah and I decided to embrace this principle, it

completely transformed not just our finances but also our hearts.

By putting God first, we experienced a freedom we never knew was possible. The freedom from fear, freedom from materialism, and freedom to trust God fully washed over our lives.

The Signs of Financial Bondage

Many Christians live in financial bondage without recognizing it. Here are some warning signs that materialism may have a hold on your life:

1. Persistent Anxiety About Money

Despite adequate income, you experience constant worry about financial matters. This anxiety reveals an unhealthy attachment to financial security.

2. Identity Tied to Possessions

Your sense of worth fluctuates based on what you own or your financial status compared to others.

3. Difficulty Giving Generously

You experience internal resistance, rationalization, or regret when giving to others or to God's work.

4. Excessive Focus on Accumulation

You find yourself constantly wanting more—the next purchase, upgrade, or experience—without experiencing lasting satisfaction.

5. Financial Secrecy or Deception

You hide purchases, debts, or financial decisions from those close to you out of shame or fear of judgment.

6. Comparison-Driven Spending

Your purchasing decisions are significantly influenced by what others have or what creates a certain impression.

7. Use of Money to Fill Emotional Voids

Shopping or spending serves as therapy or comfort during times of emotional distress.

Breaking free from these patterns begins with recognizing them and then implementing God's principles of financial freedom, starting with the tithe.

God's Ultimate Example: First and Best

God did not randomly decide He wanted our first and best. This principle was so important to God that He decided to show us exactly what He meant. He gave His best first—His Son, Jesus Christ.

Paul writes in 1 Corinthians 15:20, "But now Christ is risen from the dead and has become the firstfruits of those who have fallen asleep" (NKJV). God didn't hesitate to offer His very best to redeem humanity. Jesus is the ultimate firstfruit, demonstrating God's generosity and love for us.

When we give God our firstfruits—whether it's our time, energy, or finances—we're reflecting His heart. It's not just about following a command; it's about mirroring the sacrifice of Jesus and recognizing that everything we have ultimately comes from God. Giving God our first and best is a declaration of trust and gratitude, showing that He's at the center of our lives.

THE IDEA of giving God our first and best isn't just a suggestion; it's woven into the fabric of Scripture. Proverbs 3:9–10 teaches, "Honor the Lord with your possessions, and with the firstfruits of all your increase; so your barns will be filled with plenty, and your vats will overflow with new wine" (NKJV).

This isn't just a promise of financial blessing—it's a principle that affects every area of life. Giving God the first portion of what we have invites Him to bless the rest. It's an act of faith that says, "God, You are my provider, and I trust You completely."

In Exodus 13:2, God instructed the Israelites to consecrate their firstborn to Him: "Consecrate to Me all the firstborn; whatever opens the womb among the children of Israel, both of man and beast; it is Mine." (NKJV)

That first portion is sacred and set apart for God. When we offer our firstfruits, we're acknowledging His sovereignty over everything we have and inviting His blessings to flow into every area of our lives.

Paul reinforces this in Romans 11:16a: "For if the firstfruit is holy, the lump is also holy" (NKJV). By dedicating the first portion to God, we're consecrating everything that follows. It's a tangible way to say, "Lord, all I have is Yours, and I trust You to multiply and bless it."

Trusting God in the Valley: The Ultimate Test

I know trusting God with your first can be difficult, especially when finances are tight, or the bills are piling up.

It can feel impossible to give when there's so much need staring you in the face. But let me tell you what I've learned: God doesn't want your leftovers—He wants your trust by giving back to Him your first.

Tithing is more than a financial act; it's a spiritual declaration that says, "God, I trust You more than I trust my paycheck." And here's the amazing part—when you take that step of faith, God always shows up in ways you can't imagine.

In Malachi 3:11, God makes this promise: "And I will rebuke the devourer for your sakes, so that he will not destroy the fruit of your ground, nor shall the vine fail to bear fruit for you in the field" (NKJV). When you tithe, you're placing your resources under God's protection. He rebukes the devourer—the forces that drain your finances—and ensures that what you have is blessed and multiplied.

This isn't just about avoiding financial struggles; it's about experiencing the peace that comes from knowing God is in control. Trusting Him with your first opens the door for His provision and frees you from the grip of fear.

The Valley Seasons of Life

Valleys—those difficult seasons of financial constraint—come to everyone. It may be due to:

- Job loss or career transition
- Medical expenses or health crises
- Economic downturns
- Family emergencies
- Educational investments

•Business challenges

These valley seasons often become the proving ground for our trust in God. It's easy to tithe when abundance flows; the true test comes when resources seem scarce. Yet Scripture shows that some of the most powerful examples of tithing occurred during seasons of lack:

•The widow who gave her last two mites (Mark 12:41–44)

•The widow of Zarephath who fed Elijah from her last meal (1 Kings 17:8–16)

•The early church who shared generously despite persecution (Acts 4:32–37)

In these examples, the valley became the very place where God demonstrated His supernatural provision in response to faithful giving. The principle remains: God is most honored not by the amount we give, but by the trust we demonstrate in giving our first even when it seems impossible.

Breaking Free from the Spirit of Mammon

God gives you the tool and opportunity to break free from the slavery of materialism. Let's face it—the world we live in is obsessed with wealth and possessions. But tithing offers us a way out. It's a countercultural act that sets us free from the spirit of mammon.

Jesus reminds us in John 10:10, "The thief does not come except to steal, and to kill, and to destroy. I have come that they may have life, and that they may have it more abundantly" (NKJV). Materialism is a thief. It steals your joy, kills your peace, and distracts you from what truly matters.

When we give God our first and best, we declare that our trust isn't in money or possessions—it's in Him. Tithing isn't about losing something; it's about gaining everything that truly matters. It's about aligning your heart with God's and experiencing the abundant life He promises.

Jesus put it plainly in Matthew 6:33: "Seek first the kingdom of God and His righteousness, and all these things shall be added to you" (NKJV).

When we honor God with our firstfruits, we're putting His Kingdom first in our lives. It's not about the amount we give; it's about the heart behind it. God doesn't need your money—He wants your heart. And when you trust Him with your first, He promises to meet all your needs abundantly.

Leah and I have seen this firsthand. When we committed to tithing consistently, even during seasons of financial uncertainty, we experienced God's faithfulness in incredible ways. It wasn't always easy, but it was always worth it.

The Science of Generosity: Research Confirms Scripture

Modern scientific research continues to validate what Scripture has taught for thousands of years about generosity and giving:

Neurological Benefits

Studies using functional MRI have revealed that acts of generosity activate pleasure centers in the brain, releasing:

- **Dopamine**—The "reward" neurotransmitter
- **Serotonin**—The mood stabilizer
- **Oxytocin**—The "bonding" hormone

This phenomenon, sometimes called "helper's high," demonstrates that we are literally designed to experience joy when we give.

Psychological Benefits

Research published in *The Journal of Positive Psychology* has documented numerous psychological benefits of regular giving:

- Reduced depression symptoms
- Decreased anxiety
- Heightened sense of purpose
- Improved self-image
- Greater resilience during personal hardship

Physical Health Benefits

Multiple long-term studies have found connections between regular giving and:

- Lower blood pressure
- Reduced inflammatory markers
- Stronger immune response
- Extended longevity (up to five years in some studies)

Relational Benefits

Giving strengthens human connections through:

- Increased empathy
- Enhanced trust in communities
- Expanded social networks

• Improved relationship satisfaction

This growing body of evidence reveals an important truth: God's command to tithe and give generously isn't arbitrary—it's aligned with how He designed humans to flourish. When we follow His principles of giving, we cooperate with our created design and experience the "abundant life" Jesus promised.

Steps Not Rules: A Pathway to Financial Freedom

These aren't just rules to follow—they're steps that help you cultivate a heart of trust and obedience.

I want you to walk in the freedom of God's favor. This is not a competition. I have my relationship with God and thus I am blessed by His favor. I want you to also know all of God's goodness in your life.

Living out the Principle of First is about so much more than financial stewardship—it's about walking in the freedom of God's favor. When you trust Him with your first and best, you'll experience His blessings in every area of your life.

Honoring God with your first through the tithe shields your heart from the distractions of wealth and redirects your focus to God as your provider. It's not about what you lose— it's about the peace, purpose, and abundance you gain when you fully trust Him.

The Pathway to God's Favor: Reverent Obedience

How do you get that? The same way I did and that's by following God's Word that unlocks the blessings of His covenant provisions. The key is Reverent Obedience. You might not fully understand it yet and you may even feel a little resentment at first, but tithing, bringing to God the first tenth of your finances, is an act of obedience to honor God. Only after you show honor can God bless.

"And all the tithe of the land, whether of the seed of the land or of the fruit of the tree, is the Lord's. It is holy to the Lord (Leviticus 27:30 NKJV).

Being obedient to tithe does not force God to love you. He already does, but it does allow you the opportunity to draw closer to Him through obeying His will. Knowing and living within God's will is where His abundant favor is found. He loves us so much, He even gave us a simple blueprint for knowing His will and His way into closer relationship.

When we tithe, we remove any barriers and reflect the character of God. The favor of God is the character of God reflected in our lives. That benefits all areas like family, health, and finances.

Jesus himself gives you the instructions to unlock God's plans for your life.

Matthew 6:9—"In this manner, therefore, pray:
Our Father in heaven,

God is where? In the same place where we want the blessings to come from. Heaven—not the world.

Hallowed be Your name.

Hebrew—"qadosh"—"holy" or "sacred". Set apart, worthy of reverence.

Your kingdom come.

Asking for God's reign and rule to be established on Earth as it is in heaven. It's a request for God's perfect plan to unfold in your life.

Your will be done

God's will is that we live in alignment with Him by reflecting His divine character.

God's Garden Blueprint for life was—is—and always will be His plan for you.

"Then God blessed them, and God said to them, "Be fruitful and multiply; fill the earth and subdue it; have dominion over the fish of the sea, over the birds of the air, and over every living thing that moves on the earth" (Genesis 1:28 NKJV).

Continuing...

On earth as it is in heaven

(Matthew 6:9–10 NKJV).

How can God's will in heaven be done on earth?

You + Holy Spirit = Believer's Authority to do what?

PULL HEAVEN TO EARTH

Jesus would not have taught His disciples to pray that God's will in heaven could be done on earth if that was not possible. Do you want to pull heaven down or pull hell up? It's your choice. Choose wisely.

IT'S NEVER TOO LATE: Harold and Claire's Testimony

You might be wondering if these principles still apply if you're in a later season of life. The journey of Harold and Claire demonstrates that walking in the freedom of God's favor can begin at any age. Harold and Claire titled their testimony, "It's Never Too Late." I wrote this section for them, but these are their words.

Harold leaned forward in his chair, his voice carrying the weight of regret. "We spent forty-five years in church, always putting a little something in the offering plate, but never tithing consistently."

At seventy-two, Harold and his wife Claire were facing the limitations of a fixed income. Their modest pension and Social Security benefits covered their basic needs, but there was little room for extras—and certainly not for giving away 10 percent.

"We had always told ourselves we'd be more generous when we had more," Claire explained. "Then suddenly we were retired, and that 'more' never materialized."

The couple's perspective changed dramatically after their church offered a class on biblical finances. They calculated what a true tithe would be from their monthly income: $267.

"That first month was terrifying," Harold admitted. "We had to adjust our budget, cut back on some small luxuries. But we committed to honoring God first, even at this late stage."

WITHIN SIX MONTHS, the couple experienced something unexpected—not a financial windfall, but a profound sense of purpose and freedom.

"We realized we'd been hoarding not just our money but our gifts and time as well," Claire said. "Once we broke that spirit of scarcity by tithing, we found ourselves serving in church ministries, mentoring younger couples about marriage, and experiencing joy we hadn't known in decades."

Two years into their tithing journey, Harold and Claire have experienced modest but meaningful financial blessings —unexpected refunds, reduced medical expenses, and generous gifts from family. But they insist the true transformation has been internal.

"We wish we hadn't waited so long," Harold reflected. "We spent decades missing out on God's best because we were too afraid to test His promises. Now we tell every senior citizen we know—it's never too late to start honoring God with your first and best."

The God Guarantee: Foundation for a Blessed Life

I call it the God Guarantee. Once you commit to bringing your first to God, you will become a skilled Spirit-led kingdom caretaker of all your family, finances, possessions, business, property, and relationships. Sometimes it requires us to have skin in the game. You can't see what you are missing out on or wasting until you are willing to look at the bigger, spiritual picture of stewardship.

Healthy stewards are blessed stewards. God has given you authority to manage everything He created. How are you doing in that area of caring for all He has entrusted to you? Is the oil in your car overdue for a change? How's your health? How's your marriage? Yep, we must steward those gifts from God as well. Do you see how important it is to rely on God for helping you steward?

Every successful owner and manager team has a rock-solid relationship grounded in trust and communications. Tithing establishes the supernatural connection of trust, and prayer becomes your direct connection for knowing His will in all things. But God must be first in your life. Tithing is the first and simplest way of showing that.

A Whole-Life Stewardship Approach

The principles we apply to tithing extend to every area of life that God has entrusted to us. When we embrace whole-life stewardship, we recognize that everything belongs to God, and we are simply managing His resources. This perspective transforms:

1. Time Stewardship

Just as we give God the first portion of our finances, we can honor Him with the firstfruits of our time—beginning each day with prayer and Scripture before other activities claim our attention.

2. Talent Stewardship

Our abilities and spiritual gifts are divine deposits meant

to be invested for kingdom purposes, not hoarded or used exclusively for personal gain.

3. Relationship Stewardship

Our connections with family, friends, colleagues, and neighbors are opportunities to reflect God's character and extend His kingdom influence.

4. Physical Stewardship

Our bodies are temples of the Holy Spirit, requiring intentional care through nutrition, rest, exercise, and medical attention.

5. Environmental Stewardship

The earth and its resources are divine gifts to be carefully managed, not exploited or neglected.

6. Intellectual Stewardship

Our minds and educational opportunities are to be developed for God's glory and the service of others.

When we apply the firstfruits principle to each of these areas, we experience God's blessing in every dimension of life. Tithing becomes not an isolated financial transaction but the foundational practice of a comprehensive lifestyle of stewardship.

The big question at this point is whether God truly is first in your life. If God multiplied loaves and fishes for people who walked away after His Son taught them, imagine what He will do for those who truly fear and obey Him. It was this reality that challenged Leah and me. God simply asked us both if He was our priority.

We loved the Lord and honored Him as we felt we knew how. But, the truth was that we were not loving Him the way He asked to be loved. We had applied our own standard of natural relationship to a supernatural God.

When posed with that question, we both walked away from the heights of our careers. He was very close to our top priority, but God did not come first in our lives. We were busy building our influence in the secular world. It's easy to claim trust in God when your bank account is full.

We surrendered everything, including health insurance, free vehicles, pensions, influence, and millions of dollars annually. Yet, through honoring God with our tithe, whether we had millions or hundreds, He continues multiplying loaves and fishes.

God wants to use His relationship with you as a covenant example not just to nonbelievers, but to lukewarm Christians, that His promise of abundant favor remains as powerful today as it was when first established.

If you're ready to take that step, I encourage you to trust God with your first and best. Watch as He opens the floodgates of heaven and fills your life with His favor. Seek His Kingdom first, and everything else will follow. Step into the freedom of God's favor today.

Chapter Summary: The Four Key Takeaways

1.Breaking Financial Bondage Requires Recognition— Identifying the signs of materialism's hold is the first step toward freedom.

2.God Demonstrated the Principle of First—Jesus as the firstfruits shows that God established this principle by His own example.

3.Valley Seasons Test Our Trust—Tithing during difficult financial times demonstrates our deepest priorities and opens the door to supernatural provision.

4.Tithing Launches Whole-Life Stewardship—The principles of firstfruits extend beyond finances to every area God has entrusted to us.

CHAPTER 8
LET'S GET SERIOUS ABOUT CHEERFUL GIVING

ONE OF MY goals in sharing this teaching is to clarify according to Scripture the distinctions between tithes and giving. Too often they are used synonymously and that creates confusion even when God's Word is presented.

Giving is a gift from God that measures your true attitude of generosity. What does your giving show you about your heart?

It would be easy to avoid this area of Scripture because many Christians use the terms "giving" or "generous giver" to avoid tithing. Most truly have a desire to be generous but miss the biblical standard of what it means to give.

To remain silent because someone might be offended or disagree would be akin to cheering on a race runner when you know they are heading in the wrong direction. Let's shed God's light of understanding on this area of honoring God.

The Progression from Tithing to Giving

Bringing clarity is the best way to set the foundation of what is biblical giving from Jesus' perspective. Matthew 25:34–40 shows us that Jesus connects our actions to a deeper spiritual truth.

Giving is not about the amount but about reflecting the heart of God. When we serve others, we are serving Him. Our generosity is a direct outpouring of God's character within us.

"Then the King will say to those on his right, 'Come, you who are blessed by my Father, inherit the Kingdom prepared for you from the creation of the world. For I was hungry, and you fed me. I was thirsty, and you gave me a drink.

I was a stranger, and you invited me into your home. I was naked, and you gave me clothing. I was sick, and you cared for me. I was in prison, and you visited me.'

Then these righteous ones will reply, 'Lord, when did we ever see you hungry and feed you? Or thirsty and give you something to drink? Or a stranger and show you hospitality? Or naked and give you clothing? When did we ever see you sick or in prison and visit you?'

And the King will say, 'I tell you the truth, when you did it to one of the least of these my brothers and sisters, you were doing it to me!'"

The solid foundation upon which giving must be based is obedience. Deuteronomy 11:1 reminds us, "Therefore, you shall love the Lord your God, and keep His charge, His statutes, His judgments, and His commandments always." (NKJV)

Loving God means obeying Him. There's no Plan B.

Building on the Foundation: The Three-Level Approach

The purpose of a foundation is to build something upon it. I want you to construct a best blessed life grounded in the truth of God's Word. Once the foundation is solid, layers are placed upon it to achieve a fuller structure of building up our faith. There are three levels of scaffolding required in God's process for building up obedient and generous hearts.

The first two levels of Principle of First and the tithe have been discussed. Let's look at the third level in God's relationship-building process through obedience—giving.

"We make a living by what we get, but we make a life by what we give."

Dave Ramsey

Let's follow through on the apostle Paul's instructions in 2 Corinthians:

The Cheerful Giver

"But this I say: He who sows sparingly will also reap sparingly, and he who sows bountifully will also reap bountifully. So let each one give as he purposes in his heart, not grudgingly or of necessity; for God loves a cheerful giver.

And God is able to make all grace abound toward you, that you, always having all sufficiency in all things, may have an abundance for every good work" (2 Corinthians 9:6–8 NKJV).

The Anatomy of Cheerful Giving

Just so we are clear, Paul is not talking about tithing in this Scripture. He is talking about giving. How do we know? He says giving. He's also not talking about the amount given but the attitude of your heart toward God when you give. You should not give to God with the same attitude you pay your taxes or car insurance.

Unfortunately, 2 Corinthians 9:6–8 has become the escape pod for Christians who reject tithing either through lack of understanding Scripture or just a rebellion against God's command.

Verse 7, "So let each one give as he purposes in his heart, not grudgingly or of necessity", has been hijacked to dismiss obedience to God's command to tithe and instead do what you feel like, and only if you feel like it.

While this completely applies to giving, which is anything given above the first 10 percent, it does not replace the tithe. One is obedience and the other is generosity.

As a Christian, it should be important to reflect the character of God simply because it means we are living our lives in His will and according to His nature. Generous giving is a characteristic of God.

The Greek Perspective on Cheerful Giving

The Greek word translated as "cheerful" in 2 Corinthians 9:7 is "hilaros"—from which we get our English word "hilarious." This wasn't a mild contentment but an exuberant joy in the act of giving. Early Christians understood this to mean giving that:

- Sprang from delight rather than duty
- Created joy for both giver and recipient
- Reflected God's own joyful generosity
- Was motivated by love rather than obligation

This type of giving goes beyond tithing (the firstfruits) to a lifestyle of generosity that flows throughout all aspects of life. It's not about "how much" but "how joyfully."

GREEK INSIGHT: The term "hilaros" (cheerful) was used in secular Greek to describe festive celebrations and heartfelt hospitality. When Paul used this term for giving, he was suggesting that generosity should feel like a celebration, not an obligation.

So being generous is a big deal to God. A question I get often enough to know it brings curiosity to believers is, "How do I know if I'm being generous?" Let's look in the book.

Tithing makes it easy because the word tithe literally means, "tenth." Understanding "generous" is not as simple, but God does not leave you without examples by which to know how to quantify generosity.

Scripture sets the standard for generosity, so when you do give, you will be confident you are following God's example. Our senior elder, Scott Hulbert, explains generosity as the most natural outward expression of an inner attitude of compassion and loving kindness.

Before we jump into those examples, I want to give you a big picture of what giving looks like on a national scale. While God's abundant provision Scripturally stands on the two legs of obedience and generosity, most church-attending believers do not tithe or give.

In America, on average, about 21 percent of all Christians who attend church faithfully tithe and or give. A main source of the reluctance to give is linked to the words we use.

There are words we begin to use interchangeably over time which blurs their meanings, but their true meaning has not been diminished. I'll offer a few examples that I used in my sermon series.

What's the biblical difference between sin and iniquity?

Sin is any act that goes against God's will or moral law.

Iniquity is premeditated, continuing, and intentional sin.

EXAMPLE: David's offense with Bathsheba started as sin but became iniquity as he compounded it with deceit and murder.

What's the biblical difference between tithing and giving?

Tithing is a set 10 percent established as a principle of firstfruit offered back to God.

Giving is voluntary and is motivated by generosity.

Each has very different purposes.

The Biblical Standards of Generosity

Applying both correctly brings balance. Maintaining that balance requires understanding you cannot give as an alternative to tithe.

NOWHERE IN SCRIPTURE will you find that option for avoiding God's command. To the contrary, God makes it a condition of love.

"If you love Me, keep My commandments" (John 14:15 NKJV).

Giving can include offerings, and any other form of generosity to include money, vehicles, property, gifts, etc.

Giving can be directed to the local church and designated for a special project or purpose. Giving can be given directly to someone to help them.

Where the tithe reflects reverent fear of the Lord through obedience, giving reflects a heart of charity and love. So why do we give? God gave to us first—that's the simple answer.

"For God so loved the world that He gave His only begotten Son, that whoever believes in Him should not perish but have everlasting life" (John 3:16 NKJV).

Our giving reflects God's character:

"So, God created man in His own image; in the image of God, He created him; male and female He created them" (Genesis 1:27 NKJV).

The word "image" from this Scripture is "tselem" in the Hebrew and means a deeper reflection of God's character and attributes. Reflecting God's character goes much deeper than imitating Him. We supernaturally carry a piece of the divine within us. In His character, we are called to give as He gave.

One way of being more like God comes from the Principle of Reaping and Sowing:

"The generous will prosper;

those who refresh others will themselves be refreshed" (Proverbs 11:25 NLT).

This is a valuable distinction between the tithe and giving that I trust helps shed light on the importance between the two and understanding Scripture specific to each.

While the tithe is a set 10 percent, giving is connected to an adjustable variable. That variable is your heart for generosity.

What you sow, you reap. This does not only apply to finances. If you sow love, you will reap love. If you sow discord, you will reap chaos. I've never planted a watermelon seed and had an apple tree pop up.

Luke gives a similar witness—the same measure you give —you get back:

"Give, and it will be given to you: good measure, pressed down, shaken together, and running over will be put into your bosom. For with the same measure that you use, it will be measured back to you" (Luke 6:38 NKJV).

Have you received abundantly from God? This is where the hard truths must be addressed in your relationship with God. The question should not be, "Why has God not given to me?" The first question is, "Why haven't you first given to God?"

To answer this question, we have arrived at the illustrations or the standards of biblical generosity. There's a saying about climbing the ladder of success only to reach the top and discover it's the wrong ladder. Remember, it's not about the amount. It's about your heart.

Biblical Standards of Generosity: The Widow's Mites

Standard of Generosity One:

The Widow's Two Mites

"Now Jesus sat opposite the treasury and saw how the people put money into the treasury. And many who were rich put in much. Then one poor widow came and threw in two mites, which make a quadrans.

So, He called His disciples to Himself and said to them, 'Assuredly, I say to you that this poor widow has put in more than all those who have given to the treasury; for they all put in out of their abundance, but she out of her poverty put in all that she had, her whole livelihood'" (Mark 12:41–44 NKJV).

Are you generous if you give a "quadran"? That's the smallest Roman coin, worth about two dollars in today's value. Maybe you quickly reply, "YES!!! I'll give two bucks." But hold on.

The widow did not give two dollars, she gave what Mark 12:44 says was "out of her poverty put in all that she had, her whole livelihood."

Cambridge Dictionary defines "livelihood" as the way someone earns the money people need to pay for food, a place to live, clothing. With a show of hands, who has literally given their livelihood, every penny, your house, car, furniture, everything to God?

This is not to shame you but to show you that Jesus' example of biblical generosity is to teach you it's not about the amount—it's about the heart. You don't have to have material wealth to give generously, but you must have a heart for generosity.

Biblical Standards of Generosity: Mary's Perfume

The next standard of generosity is found in the gospel of Mark:

"And being in Bethany at the house of Simon the leper, as He sat at the table, a woman came having an alabaster flask of very costly oil of spikenard. Then she broke the flask and poured it on His head.

But there were some who were indignant among themselves, and said, 'Why was this fragrant oil wasted? For it might have been sold for more than three hundred denarii and given to the poor.' And they criticized her sharply" (Mark 14:3–5 NKJV).

Mary, who is the focus of this example of generosity, poured out a full bottle of perfume. "That's not too bad," you say. "I got an old bottle at home."

Look closer at what Scripture is saying as it relates to a standard of generous giving. Mark specifically states that the perfume equaled 300 denarii. In today's value, it equates to one year's salary.

IN 2024 THE average American income according to the US
Bureau of Labor Statistics was $61,984. Have you ever given
one year of your entire salary to God? How about leaving
your profession to serve the church full-time for one year?
For free.

I've already shared a bit of my testimony, but I'd like to
offer this as I believe it relates to generous giving. In 2015, I
was in my fifth year as a chief of police and my twenty-sixth
year of law enforcement.

Additionally, I taught college classes at the local
university and served as a subject matter expert for the
federal government. It was a busy time but my most lucrative
season.

I was four years from a full thirty-year pension with crazy
benefits such as health care and one 100 percent of my
highest years as my pension pay for life.

In August of that year, the Lord spoke so clearly and said,
"You spent your career locking men up, now live your life
setting them free." It was so impactful that two weeks later I
was a civilian for the first time in my adult life.

God did not say I'd be a pastor or plant a church. That
was all He said. I walked away from everything. Even the
cozy federal contractor job. At the time of this writing, it's
been almost ten years, and I have served the Lord full-time
and never once received a salary or health insurance. God
has, is, and will continue to provide for our family.

I ONLY OFFER this as an example that pouring it all out, whether it's perfume or your whole livelihood, is a standard you can achieve because it's the measure of your heart for God.

The Extravagant Generosity Principle

Getting back to Mary's illustration, and the distinction between tithing and giving: words matter. They can create confusion that stop believers from receiving God's abundant blessings but mostly can limit the relationship with God.

You cannot be casual or flippant about giving and declare you are generous or cheerful if you do not understand what that means. It's not based on your feelings—it is based on God's Word—all His Word from start to finish.

Mary wasn't just giving the monetary value of a year's wages. She was giving her heart! Her generosity did NOT go unnoticed by Jesus! Matthew 26:13 says, "I tell you the truth, wherever the Good News is preached throughout the world, this woman's deed will be remembered and discussed" (NLT). God always rewards giving with the right heart.

Your heart's condition toward God is vital to understand. So many self-professed believers offer lip service only. While they might enjoy the notoriety from the church leaders and other congregants, their true intentions are not veiled from our Lord.

God is to be feared, and people playing fast and loose will experience the consequences of their rebellion. There is an extreme example of this, but it was required in the early church to set the standard of taking God seriously. It's a standard that remains today.

A Warning Example: Ananias and Sapphira

There was a couple in the early church who gave abundantly, but their heart loved the amount of the money given more than God who they were giving it to.

It literally cost them their lives. A heart that chooses to love money over God brings death to the relationship with God. Let's look at the story of Ananias and his wife, Sapphira. The entire account is found in Acts 5:1–11, but I'll share the highlights for my illustration.

The couple sold a piece of property and decided to keep some of the money and give the rest to the church. Sounds great, right? Except they chose to lie about the amount and claimed they gave all the money from the sale to the church.

It was their money to do with what they pleased, so why lie? They wanted the earthly accolades of man. What they did was dishonor God through their deceptive hearts and lie to the Holy Spirit. Ananias dropped dead when confronted.

His wife suffered the same fate when questioned a little later.

"And the young men came in and found her dead, and carrying her out, buried her by her husband. So great fear came upon all the church and upon all who heard these things" (Acts 5:10–11 NKJV).

Once news spread, a holy, reverent fear of the Lord fell upon the church. I can imagine so. What do you think would happen in today's church if two people died after grieving the Holy Spirit?

Maybe you'd be surprised to know that the body of Christ did not scatter at the news of their deaths. The church became more united and powerful than before. Acts 5:12 says there was continuing power in the church, "And through the hands of the apostles many signs and wonders were done among the people. And they were all with one accord in Solomon's Porch" (NKJV).

The Key to Signs and Wonders: Holy Reverent Fear

Do Not Miss This—God's power continued in the church. Why? Because "great fear came upon all the church." Fear of the Lord is required before we can have a truly intimate relationship with Him.

Too many believers treat the Lord with a casual, nonchalant, take-Him-or-leave-Him attitude. There is a lack of holy fear of God. But when the body does come together in reverence, they see unity, signs and wonders.

Do you want to see signs and wonders in your life? They occur when we honor the Lord with our obedience to the tithe and cultivate a heart for generous giving. God moves in atmospheres of holy, reverent fear.

I'll wrap this up with the revelation the Lord first gave me about this teaching series. Recall what I said about His correction and encouragement about obedience. What Holy Spirit was sharing was the body of Christ must go all in.

PATTING ourselves on the back at 99.9 percent does not bring the power of signs and wonders. Honoring God with the tithe and generous giving opens the door for Him to multiply His power in the church and among the people—that's YOU!

God wants the lost and the lukewarm to see how He provides abundantly for His covenant family—that's YOU!

But to carry the anointing of His Signs and Wonders, we must come to Him in a Holy, Reverent Fear of God—That Must Be YOU!

That starts with obedience to His Word and reflecting His character. That character is reflected in the tithe and giving. Who wants God's power?

You are the church within which God wants to move! I challenge you as individuals and as the corporate body of the church to honor God's commands with the tithe and giving so that:

"...great fear came upon all the church" (Acts 5:11) and:

"And through the hands of the apostles many signs and wonders were done among the people. And they were all with one accord in Solomon's Porch" (Acts 5:12, NKJV).

Are you serious about cheerful giving? Work through the practical application to get a clear perspective.

MOVING FROM THEORY TO PRACTICE: Creating Your Giving Plan

Generosity, like any spiritual discipline, requires intentional practice. Here's a practical approach to developing your giving plan beyond the tithe:

Step 1: Pray for God's Direction

Begin by asking God to reveal specific areas where He wants you to give. This might include:

•Ministries that align with your spiritual gifts

•Communities or people groups He's placed on your heart

•Causes that address injustices that concern you

•Individuals in your sphere of influence with specific needs

Step 2: Budget for Generosity

After establishing your tithe (10 percent), create a separate category in your budget for offerings and giving:

•Start with a percentage that stretches but doesn't strain

•Consider setting aside funds in a dedicated "giving account"

•Plan for both regular giving and spontaneous generosity

Step 3: Cultivate an Awareness of Need

Train yourself to recognize opportunities to give:

•Ask the Holy Spirit to heighten your awareness of needs around you

•Research effective organizations in areas you feel called to support

• Build relationships with people from different socioeconomic backgrounds

• Learn about global and local needs through reliable sources

Step 4: Give Strategically and Joyfully

Make your giving both intentional and heartfelt:

• Seek to maximize impact rather than just emotional satisfaction

• Balance spontaneous giving with planned, consistent support

• Look for opportunities where your unique skills/resources can be leveraged

• Celebrate the privilege of participating in God's work through giving

Step 5: Evaluate and Adjust

Periodically review your giving practice:

• Has your giving been joyful or obligatory?

• Are you seeing fruit from your investments?

• Are there new areas where God is calling you to give?

• How has your capacity for generosity grown?

Remember, the goal is not to reach a specific dollar amount or percentage, but to develop a heart that increasingly reflects God's generosity. Each step toward greater giving should be motivated by love, not guilt or obligation.

CHAPTER SUMMARY: The Four Key Takeaways

1.Tithing and Giving Serve Different Purposes—Tithing is about obedience; giving is about generosity. Both are essential to spiritual growth.

2.Biblical Generosity Is Measured by Heart, Not Amount—The examples of the widow and Mary show that God values sacrificial giving that flows from love.

3.Deception in Giving Brings Judgment—Ananias and Sapphira demonstrate the seriousness with which God views our heart's condition in giving.

4.Holy Fear Precedes Supernatural Power—When the church honors God with reverent obedience, the stage is set for signs and wonders to follow.

CONCLUSION
THE JOURNEY OF OBEDIENT BLESSINGS

The journey we've taken together through these pages isn't simply about financial principles—it's about a profound invitation to experience God at His Word.

When we choose to honor Him through our tithes and offerings, we're not just following rules; we're stepping into a divine covenant relationship that transforms every aspect of our lives.

Remember that God doesn't need your money—He wants your heart. The tithe is His divine test that reveals whether material possessions have a hold on you or whether your trust truly rests in Him. It's the cornerstone of a life built on faith rather than fear, abundance rather than scarcity.

The Relationship-Trust-Blessing Framework Revisited

As we conclude this journey, let's return to the Relationship-Trust-Blessing framework we introduced at the beginning:

1.**RELATIONSHIP:** Tithing begins and ends with relationship. The goal has never been about funding religious institutions but about deepening your connection with God.

2.**TRUST:** Through the act of tithing, you've demonstrated trust in God's provision, establishing the foundation for growth in every area of life.

3.**BLESSING:** As you honor God with your firstfruits, He releases blessing in three dimensions—material, spiritual, and relational—creating a holistic transformation.

4.**INCREASED CAPACITY:** These blessings expand your capacity for both receiving and giving, which deepens your relationship with God, continuing the upward spiral of faith.

I've walked this path from resistance to revelation, and I can testify that God's promises are not empty words. They are living truths that manifest when we step out in obedient faith. The windows of heaven truly do open when we bring our whole tithe to the storehouse.

Your Invitation to the 90-Day Challenge

Today, I extend this challenge: Test God in this. It's the only area of Scripture where He explicitly invites such a test. For the next three months, commit to honoring God with your firstfruits through consistent tithing.

Watch how He works—not just in your finances, but in your faith. Document the changes, celebrate the victories, and witness His faithfulness unfold.

The choice is yours. Will you continue to serve the god of materialism, or will you step into the freedom of trusting your Heavenly Father? Will you settle for what you can provide yourself, or will you unlock the supernatural abundance that comes only through obedience?

God invites us to test Him in this area of tithing. God is waiting to demonstrate His faithfulness. Your act of reverent obedience through tithing and generous giving opens the door to His miraculous provision. Don't miss another day of the abundant life He has designed for you.

The windows of heaven are waiting to be unlocked. The key to obedience is in your hands. I offer you a rock-solid process for encountering God at a level you have yet to experience. The 90-Day Tithing Challenge is what I used when I had my first major relationship breakthrough with the Lord. I ask that you trust Him more than your money and put Him to the test!

Check out Appendix One for the 90-Day Tithing Challenge.

I've added a recap as Appendix Two that covers the common objections to tithing and their biblical response as a ready resource in the event you start to waver on the 90-Day Tithing Challenge. I want you to win by growing a deep, loving relationship with God.

Dr. Scott Silverii is a son of the Living God. Thankful for the gift of his wife, Leah, their kids, sons-in-law, grand-baby and more on the way, he serves to equip Godly leaders for ungodly times.

A highly decorated, twenty-five-year law enforcement career promptly ended in retirement when God called Scott out of public service and into His service. The "Chief" admits that leading people to Christ is more exciting than the twelve years he spent undercover, sixteen years in SWAT, and five years as chief of police combined.

Scott has earned postdoctoral hours in a Doctor of Ministry degree in addition to a Master of Public Administration and a Ph.D. in Cultural Anthropology. Education and experience allow for a deeper understanding in ministering to the wounded, as he worked to break free from his own past pain and abuse.

In 2016, God set Scott on a servant's path that led to planting Five Stones Church. He still serves as senior pastor and continues to write, guest speak and disciple Godly leaders for ungodly times.

ALSO BY SCOTT SILVERII

Big Book of Marriage

Favored Not Forgotten: Embrace the Season, Thrive in Obscurity, Activate Your Purpose

Unbreakable: From Past Pain To Future Glory

Retrain Your Brain - Using Biblical Meditation To Purify Toxic Thoughts

God Made Man - Discovering Your Purpose and Living an Intentional Life

Captive No More - Freedom From Your Past of Pain, Shame and Guilt

Broken and Blue: A Policeman's Guide To Health, Hope, and Healing

Life After Divorce: Finding Light In Life's Darkest Season

Police Organization and Culture: Navigating Law Enforcement in Today's Hostile Environment

The ABCs of Marriage: Devotional and Coloring Book

Love's Letters (A Collection of Timeless Relationship Advice from Today's Hottest Marriage Experts)

A First Responder Devotional

40 Days to a Better Firefighter Marriage

40 Days to a Better Military Marriage

40 Days to a Better Corrections Officer Marriage

40 Days to a Better 911 Dispatcher Marriage

40 Days to a Better EMT Marriage

40 Days to a Better Police Marriage

APPENDIX ONE: THE GOD GUARANTEE - YOUR 90-DAY TITHING JOURNEY

Taking the Tithing Challenge

I've shared my journey from resistance to revelation. I've laid out what Scripture says about tithing, addressing the most common objections.

I've explained the difference between tithing and giving, and I've shown you how God's Principle of First transforms more than just your finances.

But here's the thing—information without application is just education. God doesn't want informed Christians; He wants transformed Christians.

That's why I'm issuing a challenge directly from Scripture. In Malachi 3:10, God Himself says, "Test me in this." It's the only place in the Bible where God explicitly invites you to put Him to the test. He's so confident in His faithfulness that He literally says, "Try Me now in this" when it comes to tithing.

I call this the God Guarantee. It's not my guarantee—it's His. And today, I'm inviting you to take Him up on it.

The 90-Day Tithing Challenge

This challenge is simple but life changing. For the next ninety days, I want you to commit to bringing your full tithe faithfully to God—no compromise, no excuses, no holdbacks. Give God your first and best and watch what He does in response.

Why ninety days? Because true transformation takes time. A weekend decision can fade by Monday morning. A month might not be enough to see God's provision unfold. But ninety days gives God time to show up in your life in ways you can't explain away as coincidence.

Here's how the challenge works:

Days 1–30: Breaking the Chains

Your Commitment: Calculate exactly what your tithe is (10 percent of your gross income) and commit to giving it first —before any other expenses. If you're paid weekly or biweekly, this means bringing your tithe with each paycheck.

What to Expect: This first month might be the hardest. You'll likely face doubts. The enemy will throw every reason at you to stop. Financial pressures might make you want to hold back. This is normal! That's exactly why tithing is such a powerful trust test.

Your Milestone Goal: By day thirty, you will have established a new habit of giving God your first and best. You may or may not have seen tangible financial blessing yet, but you've taken a stand of faith that says, "God, I trust You more than my bank account."

Action Steps:

1. Calculate your exact tithe amount for each paycheck

2. Schedule your giving (online, check, or cash) to happen immediately after you're paid

3. Start a "Blessing Journal" to record both challenges and provisions

4. When you face the urge to withhold your tithe, pause and pray instead

5. Memorize Malachi 3:10

Days 31–60: Developing Trust

Your Commitment: Continue your faithful tithing but now add intentional prayer over your finances. Each time you tithe, pray specifically for God to show you areas where you can be a better steward of what remains.

What to Expect: By this phase, the initial resistance often begins to fade. You may notice subtle changes in your financial situation—unexpected provision, reduced expenses, or simply a greater peace about money. You'll likely begin recognizing God's hand in areas you previously attributed to luck or coincidence.

Your Milestone Goal: By day sixty, tithing should feel less like a sacrifice and more like a privilege. Your perspective on money will begin shifting from scarcity to abundance, regardless of your actual balance.

Action Steps:

1.   Review your spending from the first thirty days and identify any changes

2.   Look for wasteful expenses you can eliminate (the "devourer" at work)

3.   Continue documenting God's provision in your Blessing Journal

4.   Share your experience with one trusted friend

5.   Pray specifically over any financial challenges you're facing

6.   Memorize Philippians 4:19

Days 61–90: Walking in Freedom

Your Commitment: As you complete the final month, maintain your tithing commitment while beginning to explore giving beyond the tithe. Ask God if there are specific offerings He's calling you to give.

What to Expect: This is where many people experience breakthrough. The test becomes a testimony. The sacrifice becomes a source of joy. You'll likely have specific stories of God's provision that you couldn't have engineered yourself.

Your Milestone Goal: By day ninety, you should have clear evidence of God's faithfulness in your life—not necessarily that you've become wealthy, but that you've experienced His provision in ways that build your faith. You'll complete the challenge with a decision about whether tithing will become your permanent financial foundation.

Action Steps:

1. Complete a comprehensive review of the entire ninety-day period

2. Document specific examples of God's provision during the challenge

3. Prayerfully consider what offering (beyond the tithe) God might be calling you to give

4. Share your testimony with someone who is skeptical about tithing

5. Make a written commitment about your tithing future

6. Memorize 2 Corinthians 9:8

Tracking Your Journey

To make this challenge effective, you need to document what happens. Below is a simple tracking sheet you can use, or you can create your own journal.

Weekly Check-In Template

Week #: _____ **Dates:** _____

Tithe amount this week: $_____

Current financial challenges: _____
Specific prayer requests regarding finances:

_____

God's provision this week (expected and unexpected):

_____

Insights or perspective shifts: _____

Scripture that encouraged me: _____

30-Day Milestone Reflection
Date: _____

What has been the biggest challenge so far?

_____

What unexpected blessing have I experienced?

_____

How has my perspective on money changed?

_____

Am I seeing evidence of God "rebuking the devourer" in my finances? _____

Do I still believe I can't afford to tithe? Why or why not?

_____

What Scripture has become more meaningful to me?

_____

60-Day Milestone Reflection
Date: _____

How has the challenge of tithing changed from the first thirty days? _____

What consistent patterns of provision have I noticed?

_____

Has my spending changed in other areas? How?

_____

What fears about tithing have been addressed?

_____

What am I learning about God's character through this experience? _____

Who have I shared my tithing journey with?

_____

90-Day Completion Testimony
Date: _____

Summarize your ninety-day tithing journey:

_____

List specific examples of God's provision:

_____

How has your relationship with God changed through this process? _____

What have you learned about money and its role in your life?

_____

Will you continue tithing? Why or why not?

_____

What would you tell someone who is considering tithing but afraid to start? _____

When the Ninety Days Are Complete

At the end of your ninety-day journey, you'll face a decision: Will tithing become your financial foundation going forward?

I can't make that choice for you. But based on my experience and the testimonies of countless others who have taken this challenge, I'm confident I know what your answer will be.

God isn't asking you to test Him so He can show off. He's inviting you to test Him so you can experience firsthand that He is trustworthy with your whole life, including your finances.

The windows of heaven are waiting to be unlocked. The key is in your hands. Will you use it?

90-Day Tithing Challenge Commitment Card

THE GOD GUARANTEE—PUT HIM TO THE TEST
My Covenant with God

"I, _____, commit to bringing my full tithe faithfully to God for the next ninety days. I will trust Him completely as my provider and put His promise in Malachi 3:10 to the test.

I understand this is not a formula for getting rich, but an opportunity to experience God's faithfulness and provision in my life. I will document His provision and blessings during this time.

If, after ninety days of faithful tithing, I can honestly say I have not experienced God's provision and blessing, I will reevaluate this practice. But I enter this challenge expecting God to be true to His Word."

Starting date: _____ Ending date: _____

Signature: _____ Witness: _____

APPENDIX TWO:
ADDRESSING COMMON
OBJECTIONS TO TITHING

If you've spent any time in church circles discussing tithing, you've likely heard passionate arguments against it. I know these objections intimately—I once championed many of them myself.

Let's tackle head-on the most common objections we hear from sincere believers who struggle with tithing.

My goal isn't to win an argument but to clear away obstacles that might be keeping you from experiencing God's full blessing. As we examine each objection, I invite you to approach with an open heart, testing each perspective against Scripture.

I can only share what God says, so it's your opportunity and option to seek the Holy Spirit's guidance.

Objection #1: "Tithing was only part of the Old Testament law that no longer applies to Christians."

This is perhaps the most common objection I hear—and once made myself. The argument goes that tithing was part of the Mosaic law, and since Christians are under grace rather than law, tithing is no longer required.

The Biblical Response: While tithing was indeed incorporated into the law, it predates the law by hundreds of years. As we saw in Chapter 2, Abraham tithed to Melchizedek (Genesis 14:18–20) at least 430 years before the law was given to Moses. Jacob also committed to tithing (Genesis 28:20–22) long before the law was established.

Jesus himself acknowledged the practice of tithing while emphasizing the importance of justice, mercy, and faith:

"Woe to you, teachers of the law and Pharisees, you hypocrites! You give a tenth of your spices—mint, dill and cumin. But you have neglected the more important matters of the law—justice, mercy and faithfulness. You should have practiced the latter, without neglecting the former" (Matthew 23:23 NIV).

Notice Jesus didn't say, "Stop tithing." He said the Pharisees should practice justice, mercy, and faithfulness without neglecting tithing.

The early church continued patterns of radical generosity that often exceeded the tithe. While the New Testament doesn't command tithing specifically, Jesus did uphold principles of systematic, proportional giving that honors God with our firstfruits.

Objection #2: "The New Testament teaches cheerful giving, not obligatory tithing."

Many point to 2 Corinthians 9:7 ("Each of you should give what you have decided in your heart to give, not reluctantly or under compulsion, for God loves a cheerful giver" NKJV) as evidence that we should give as we feel led rather than following a percentage.

The Biblical Response: The Bible clearly distinguishes between tithing and giving. Tithing is bringing to God what already belongs to Him—the first tenth. Giving refers to offerings beyond the tithe.

The passage in 2 Corinthians is specifically addressing a special collection for the Jerusalem church during a famine —not regular giving or tithing. Paul is teaching about voluntary offerings beyond regular giving. The principle of cheerful giving doesn't negate the practice of tithing any more than the command to love negates the command not to steal. These are complementary, not contradictory, teachings.

Instead of using "cheerful giving" as an excuse to give less, we should see it as an invitation to give generously beyond the tithe with the right heart attitude.

Objection #3: "Tithing promotes a prosperity gospel that God will make me wealthy if I give."

Some worry that teaching tithing feeds into a "name it and claim it" prosperity theology that reduces God to a cosmic vending machine.

The Biblical Response: Biblical tithing is about faithfulness, not formulas. God does promise blessing to those who tithe (Malachi 3:10), but those blessings aren't always financial and certainly don't guarantee wealth.

The blessings that come from tithing include:

- Freedom from the grip of materialism
- Enhanced trust in God's provision
- The joy of participating in God's work
- Spiritual protection from the "devourer"
- God's supernatural multiplication of what remains

Many faithful tithers never become wealthy by worldly standards but experience God's provision in remarkable ways. The goal of tithing isn't to get rich but to acknowledge God's ownership and provision in our lives.

Objection #4: "I can't afford to tithe with my current financial situation."

This practical objection often comes from sincere believers facing genuine financial challenges—single parents, those with significant medical bills, people struggling with debt, or those living on fixed incomes.

The Biblical Response: This concern reflects a fundamental misunderstanding about tithing. Tithing isn't about what we can afford—it's about putting God first and trusting Him as our provider.

Remember the widow Jesus commended in Mark 12:41–44? She gave from her poverty, not her abundance. In God's economy, tithing isn't a luxury for the financially comfortable—it's a fundamental practice of faith for every believer.

When we withhold the tithe because we "can't afford it," we're saying we don't trust God to fulfill His promises to provide for our needs. We're choosing to trust in our own provision rather than God's.

As we saw in Sarah's story, tithing during financial hardship often becomes the pathway to God's provision, not an obstacle to it. God invites us to test Him in this area precisely because He knows we struggle to trust Him with our finances.

Objection #5: "Churches mismanage money, so I give to other causes instead."

Some believers have witnessed financial mismanagement or even abuse in churches, leading them to redirect their giving to parachurch organizations or direct charity instead.

The Biblical Response: While this concern can be legitimate, Scripture is clear that the tithe belongs in the "storehouse" (Malachi 3:10)—which for New Testament believers is the local church where they are spiritually fed.

If you have serious concerns about financial integrity in your church, the solution isn't to withhold your tithe but to:

1.   Respectfully address your concerns with church leadership

2.   Request transparency in financial reporting

3.   If necessary, find a church that demonstrates biblical financial stewardship

Remember that your tithe isn't ultimately going to a pastor or building fund—it's going to God. He remains faithful even when humans fall short.

As for giving to other causes, this is where offerings (beyond the tithe) come in. After honoring God with your tithe to your local church, you're free to direct additional giving to any ministry or cause God lays on your heart.

Objection #6: "The 10 percent standard was for an agricultural society and doesn't translate to modern economics."

Some argue that since the biblical tithe was primarily agricultural, the 10 percent standard doesn't directly apply to today's wage-based economy.

The Biblical Response: While the form of wealth has changed, the principle remains the same. The tithe was always about the firstfruits of increase—whether from crops, flocks, or other sources of wealth.

In our context, income has replaced agricultural yield as the primary form of increase, but the principle of honoring God with the first tenth remains unchanged. If anything, our modern financial systems make percentage-based giving easier to calculate and implement.

Throughout biblical history, God's people adapted tithing practices to their changing economic circumstances without abandoning the underlying principle. From Abraham's tithe of war spoils to the Israelites' agricultural tithes to the monetary contributions in Jesus' day, the consistent thread is honoring God with the first portion.

Objection #7: "I give in other ways—through service, hospitality, etc."

Some believers argue that they "tithe" through volunteering, hosting, or using their talents for the kingdom, suggesting that financial giving is just one way to honor God.

The Biblical Response: Service and financial giving are both important but not interchangeable. Jesus himself made this distinction when He said, "Give to Caesar what belongs to Caesar, and give to God what belongs to God" (Matthew 22:21 NLT).

While God certainly values the giving of our time and talents, these don't replace financial giving any more than financial giving replaces the need to serve. Each form of stewardship reveals different aspects of our heart toward God.

Financial giving often touches a nerve because money is one of the most tangible expressions of our priorities and trust. Jesus taught that "where your treasure is, there your heart will be also" (Matthew 6:21), highlighting the unique spiritual significance of how we handle money.

Objection #8: "Tithing is just churches trying to get my money."

Perhaps the most cynical objection comes from those who see tithing as a manipulative fundraising tactic rather than a biblical principle.

The Biblical Response: While some churches have certainly misused tithing teachings for financial gain, this abuse doesn't invalidate the biblical principle. The question isn't whether some have taught tithing with wrong motives, but whether tithing itself is biblical.

The tithe wasn't invented by modern churches seeking funds—it's been God's design since the earliest biblical accounts. Before church buildings, staff salaries, or ministry programs existed, God established the principle of the tithe as a way for His people to honor Him and support His work.

Rejecting a biblical principle because of how some have misused it would be like rejecting prayer because some have prayed hypocritically. The solution isn't to abandon the practice but to return to its pure biblical foundation.

Moving Forward in Faith

As we've examined these common objections, I hope you've seen that the biblical case for tithing stands strong. Many of the arguments against tithing stem from misunderstandings of Scripture or, more often, from the struggle to trust God with our finances.

This isn't about legalism or manipulation—it's about aligning our hearts with God's design. If you've held some of these objections, as I have in the past, I encourage you to prayerfully reconsider whether they stand up to the full counsel of Scripture.

Now that you've seen how tithing becomes the foundation for overcoming the fear that often masquerades as theological objection, I invite you to move from resistance to obedience. When we do, we discover that tithing isn't a burden but a pathway to freedom.

Reflection Questions:

1.   Which of these objections have you personally struggled with? What new perspective did you gain from examining it?

2.   If you were to set aside objections and begin tithing faithfully, what fears would you need to overcome?

3.   Ask God to reveal any areas where you've allowed intellectual arguments to mask heart issues regarding finances and trust.

www.ingramcontent.com/pod-product-compliance
Lightning Source LLC
LaVergne TN
LVHW052027080426
835513LV00018B/2195